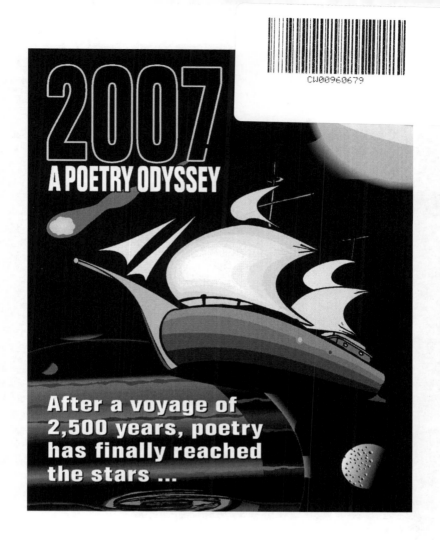

2007
A POETRY ODYSSEY

After a voyage of 2,500 years, poetry has finally reached the stars ...

Verses From Lancashire
Edited by Dave Thomas

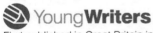 Young**Writers**

First published in Great Britain in 2007 by:
Young Writers
Remus House
Coltsfoot Drive
Peterborough
PE2 9JX
Telephone: 01733 890066
Website: www.youngwriters.co.uk

SB ISBN 978-1 84602 824 3

Foreword

This year, the Young Writers' *2007: A Poetry Odyssey* competition proudly presents a showcase of the best poetic talent selected from thousands of up-and-coming writers nationwide.

Young Writers was established in 1991 to promote the reading and writing of poetry within schools and to the young of today. Our books nurture and inspire confidence in the ability of young writers and provide a snapshot of poems written in schools and at home by budding poets of the future.

The thought, effort, imagination and hard work put into each poem impressed us all and the task of selecting poems was a difficult but nevertheless enjoyable experience.

We hope you are as pleased as we are with the final selection and that you and your family continue to be entertained with *2007: A Poetry Odyssey Verses From Lancashire* for many years to come.

Contents

Cansfield High School

Jess Day (13)	38
Daniel Crabtree (14)	39
Claire Pritchard (13)	40
Michael Lavelle (13)	41
Andrew Yates (13)	42
Hayley Evans (12)	43
Craig Hughes (12)	44
Chris Black (12)	45
Jessica Price (12)	46
Toni Andrew (12)	47
Ryan Dutton (13)	48
Charlotte Pilling (12)	49
Robbie Smyth (13)	50
Demi-Sue Roberts (11)	51
Lauren Woodford (11)	52
Josh Pearce (13)	53
Rebecca Sands (12)	54
Melanie Edwards (12)	55
Jack Ross (12)	56
Kathryn Whittle (12)	57
Ben Scott (12)	58
Kerry Charnock (12)	59
Jamie Cook (13)	60

Castlebrook High School

Mikki Wright (13)	61
Jennifer Butler (13)	62
Elizabeth Mitchell (13)	63
Daniel Whatmough (13)	64
David Meehan (13)	65
Peter Harris (13)	66
Tom Connolly (14)	67
Charlotte McDonald (13)	68
Amy Fielder (13)	69
Dominic Comrie (14)	70
Lewis Thelwell (13)	71
Danielle Leigh (14)	72
Kamo Kupi (14)	73
Laura Clough (13)	74
Andrew Gregoriou (13)	75

Jessica Endacott (14)   76
Paige Edwards (13)   77
Emma Birtles (13)   78
Andrew Garner (14)   79
Henry Hudnott (13)   80
Abbi Davies (14)   82
Jessica Szpak (13)   83
Emily Owen (12)   84
James Wharmby (12)   85

Hutton Grammar School
Michael Cafferkey (11)   86
Mark Gowdy (11)   87
Ashley Clitheroe (11)   88
William Powley (11)   89
Andy Irwin (17)   90
Philip Burns (11)   91
Sam Rigby (15)   92
Peter Tipping (11)   93

Larches House Hostel School
Jodie Parker (15)   94

Little Lever School Specialist Language College
Alex Leigh (11)   95
Cole Bradley (11)   96
Aylish Doherty (11)   97
Laura Hinchliffe (14)   98
Hannah Wallwork (14)   99
Rebecca Marsden (14)   100
Nadia Bourka (14)   101
Nicole Darbyshire (14)   102
Jennie Carter (14)   103
Hannah Westwood (11)   104
Elyse Taylor (12)   105
Jade Harrison (13)   106
Connor Peploe (12)   107
Aimee Fishwick (14)   108
Chelsey Raby (13)   109
Natasha Jamieson (12)   110
Lauren Roberts (15)   111

Rebecca Gent (13)	112
Jessica Baird (13)	113
Sarah Gee (14)	114
Sajjad Pervez (11)	115
Kaya Smith (13)	116
Rebecca Rothwell (13)	117
Axl Thomas (13)	118
Jennifer Mort (15)	119
Mark Chodacki (13)	120

Lostock Hall Community High School

Luke Brown (13)	121
Phillip Cook (13)	122
Amy Finch (13)	123
Sara-Louise Kelly (13)	124
Abbie Dawson (13)	125
Josh Blakeston (13)	126
Jade Taylor (12)	127
Matthew Tomlinson (13)	128
Tom Smith (13)	129
Lindsey Parker (12)	130
Alexandra Jackson (12)	131
Rebecca Farrell (13)	132
Chelsey Roxburgh (14)	133
Rebecca Gidley (12)	134
David Lonsdale (12)	135
Rachael Taylor (13)	136
Lewis Miller (14)	137
Michael Holland (12)	138
Alex Cairns (13)	139
Ryan McManus (13)	140
Kirstyn Winder (14)	141
Emma-Louise Jedliczka (14)	142
Gemma Crook (13)	143
Kimberley Rowe (13)	144
Rhianne Lealman (13)	145
Georgina Chelton (13)	146
Philip Whiteside (14)	147
Heather Kaylow (14)	148
Daniel Walkingshaw (14)	149
Craig Campbell (13)	150

The Poems

Close To Death

All I can hear is the sirens screeching loud
I can barely open my eyes, but what I see is the scampering crowd.

I hear clinking and clanging, what could it be?
As they lift me, my head is thumping and shooting pains inside me.

I drift in and out of consciousness, when I wake I can hear a beeping sound,
It takes me a few minutes to realise, I am no longer on the ground.

As I recovered I didn't know what went on,
So I questioned and questioned, they then told me to cross carefully from now on.

Alex James (13)
Byrchall High School

A Selection Of Seasonal Haiku

Spring
New buds on the trees
Lambs frolicking in the fields
With spring comes new life.

Summer
Blazing sun above
Slop! Slop! Ice cream on the floor
Children crying now.

Autumn
Crisp leaves falling down
The mornings are darkening
Autumn days are here.

Winter
Snowflakes floating down
Gently covering treetops
Blanketing the ground.

Kym Neil (13)
Byrchall High School

That's It, The End!

I paced across the floor,
My heartbeat raced,
Nothing mattered anymore,
The footsteps echoed,
Throughout the hall.
It didn't matter that I was armed,
So were they.
'They're here,' shouted Mary.
That was it,
It was all over,
I collapsed,
The pain controlled me,
My blood merged with Mary's.
That was it, the end,
I'd been hit,
The last words
As one sees his own death,
'Mum,' I call,
That's it, I'm dead!

Andrew Murray (12)
Byrchall High School

The Black World

Deep in the dark world of space
There is no life outside here,
The stars twinkle and the planets are dull
You can occasionally see the shooting stars.

The nine planets look so small
Even smaller than a newborn baby,
You float around in the cockpit
Even bump into the thick padded wall.

There may be planets undiscovered
More will be revealed once they are uncovered
People look for life on Mars
They could be like us humans driving in cars.

I can hear the rockets set off for space
I can see the rocket fuel burning
It takes off for an odyssey in space
The spacemen's journey to Mars awaits.

Stephen Leyland (13)
Byrchall High School

Phantom Light

I sailed a ship one moonlit night
Something strange gave me a fright,
I got out of bed and opened the door
It will scar me for life for what I saw.

I saw it disappear and then in a flash reappear
I rubbed my eyes twice to check if I was right,
Or whether it was the moonlight ruining my sight.

As I followed it in a staring trance
Me and him began to dance,
When I looked down I was floating in the air
And when I looked up I was dancing with a bear.

Charlotte Bassnett (12)
Byrchall High School

Emptiness

Feeling like my life lacks purpose, like I need a reason
See I've been feeling like a part of my life is missing
Which I can't describe to no one, or put into speech
I got a lot of stuff I like, yet there is something I need
People understand what I mean but not what I'm feeling
I got talent and friends yet I feel there is nothing I bring
And the problem isn't money I can get plenty of that
But it's useless to me so what is the point in that?
I don't need counselling, I don't need to shed my tears
All I need is a single moment to get out of here
This mental prison there's no bars yet I'm trapped and provoked
And no one feels my pain, you can't understand what I've wrote
I lack something I need and I know it's something inside
But I haven't got to write about it that's a cause of my pride
I feel like everything I do in my life is always done in vain
Why is it that everything in this world seems to cause pain?
I'm not depressed, understand this don't get my words mistaken
Feelings always there that there isn't anything that I can do
So I choose poetry to get my point of view across to you.

Adam Cunliffe (12)
Byrchall High School

Money Mission

The captain said to his men,
'Right, listen up then
We've a serious mission
Without any omission,
That we all must go into space'
So he put on his serious face
And said, 'Men, this is not a race
We must fly to Mars,
And collect it in jars
Then sell it in a foreign place.'

Sam Robinson (12)
Byrchall High School

Darkness

When you look around
What do you see?
When I look around
I see darkness.

Darkness is a hole
As empty as can be,
No colour no light,
No people I can see.

Black is the world,
Through my eyes,
You can see colour
Through your eyes.

I would give anything
To see the world again,
To see my family
And to see my friends.

But I will never see again
Not even the stars in the sky,
For that dreadful day
When I fell to the ground.

For I was blinded
From that day on,
I will never see again,
It's a world of total darkness.

April McGoldrick (12)
Byrchall High School

The Victim

You see him in the corridor,
Hiding from his doom,
Hiding from the bullies,
Who swallow him in gloom.

In nearly every lesson,
He gets cornered in his seat,
He looks into their beady eyes,
He knows this is defeat.

Everyone stares at breaktime,
He's always on his own,
He's scared of all the bullies
Who make him moan and groan.

He then sits near the teacher,
So the bullies don't come near,
But deep, deep down inside him,
His heart is still pure fear.

When the lunch bell rings,
He knows he cannot cope,
So he hides away from the bullies,
To try and find some hope.

He sits there in the toilets,
Crying for his mum,
But he knows the bullies are out there,
And his doom is yet to come.

Stephanie Cunliffe (12)
Byrchall High School

Space

In the deep of the darkness,
Where no flame burns,
In the lonely emptiness,
Floating alone.

Where the tiniest light,
Can burn you to death,
And the prettiest sight,
Sucks you inside.

If you saw what's here,
And were as lonely as this,
You would know what this is,
But what can it be?

Balls of light,
Flying here and there,
There is no height,
Only holes of death that spit you out.

Dangers are everywhere,
But no one here to help,
No one to share this scare,
No one to pull you out.

If you saw these sights,
And were scared like this,
You would know where this is,
But where can it be?

Abigail Mills (12)
Byrchall High School

What Was This Thing Down Below?

An underwater odyssey was what I had today,
I was swimming in the sea
When a little fish came my way.

He said his name was Joe,
He asked me if I know,
What this thing was down below.

I said I would drown,
If I swam deep down,
To see what this thing was down below.

He gave me some pills,
Then I grew some gills,
So that I could see what this thing was down below.

I swam down deep,
Into a little creek,
To see what this thing was down below.

To my surprise,
Right in front of my eyes,
The thing was there no more.

Jessie Johnstone (12)
Byrchall High School

The Journey

The ship set sail upon the sea
A sea of sky it meant to be
A heroic voyage into the deep
But for one thing we had to keep.

The Mumbai scrolls we had to take
To the plane called Dudrake
A fierce planet good in battle
The army made of psycho cattle.

Will the captain be a hero
Or will he return a pathetic zero?
Nervous as the darkness comes
Good luck to captain me!

Ryan West (12)
Byrchall High School

Ice Storm

The ship sliced through the icy sea,
The frozen rudder struggling free.
Some birds swooped low and swiftly past,
Most just nesting on the giant mast.
The storm was wild, the sky was black,
There was something wrong, but there was no going back.

Once more the lightning lashed its tails,
This time straight through the windswept sails.
The sail fell on deck in a fiery blaze,
Causing nothing to see but a smoky haze.
The mast gave an almighty creek,
Then smashed the hull making a tremendous leak.

The water came in as an enormous wave,
I stood my ground strong and brave.
The fire ceased and smoked and hissed,
Leaving behind an epic shroud of mist.
The ship was wrecked, I admitted defeat,
I climbed some driftwood and took my seat.,
The ship sank down and hit the rocks with a rattle
I drifted away, from the heat of battle.

Nathan Mansell (12)
Byrchall High School

The Ocean

In the ocean there are lots of fish
Eating algae from a dish
The plants are swaying side by side
Then the children take a dive
The children swim all around
Taking a tour touching the ground
Then a shark comes along
Gobbling you up with its tongue
Taking a tour of the sea
Then going home and eating their tea.

Elainor Davies (11)
Byrchall High School

My Life

My brother has gone,
He is all grown up,
Studying at university,
He is living it up.

I am still here,
Just me and my mum,
The house is so quiet,
Just the dog for fun.

On Saturday teatime,
The house comes alive,
To the sound of his music,
His deep laugh and Xbox live.

By Sunday lunch he gets out of bed,
He is tired and grumpy and argues a lot,
When I think about it, that's what I miss,
But do you know what I realised, midweek is bliss!

Thomas McLean (13)
Byrchall High School

Adulthood Sux

I don't wanna grow up,
I don't wanna be old,
Bein' an adult's not easy,
So I've been told.

I wanna stay young
And play all day,
I don't wanna grow up
And earn my pay.

It's easy to get up
And go to school,
To learn and play
And act the fool.

Going to work,
Seems boring and dumb,
I don't wanna grow up
And be like my mum.

I wanna stay young,
So I can roll in the muck,
I don't wanna grow old,
Having to clean and to cook.

Bein' a kid
Is so great and fine,
I wish I could stay this way
All the time.

Daniel Fields (13)
Byrchall High School

Do You Have A Heart?

The sun was beating down on my back,
The heat was burning my skin,
My bones were aching in agony,
I just wish I could play and make a din.

The sack of bricks was weighing me down
And my feet were covered with mud,
Scratches and bruises all over my body
And I was drowning in my own blood.

I'm thirteen years old and live in Africa,
I work all day just to survive,
Whereas on the other side of the world,
Normal teenagers get to live their lives.

I'm fourteen and live in England,
I go to school every weekday,
It's just been my birthday and I got a new games' console,
Because I needed something new to play.

I got this leaflet through the door today,
Something about people who are poor,
How they've got no food or clean water,
Like people in Africa who need more.

It doesn't matter, I don't care,
I've got money and food to eat,
They'll survive, they'll be alright,
As long as they can stand on two feet.

Do you ignore it or do you care?
Help others today as it's only fair!

Barbara Grant (13)
Byrchall High School

A Poem About Paris Hilton

Her face shines out like a gleaming star,
Her long blonde hair sways in the breeze,
She is one of the prettiest people by far,
Her light blue-eyed stare makes me freeze.

Her perfect, model-like figure
Looks great in any designer dress,
All the jealous people can only snigger
As she is never seen a mess.

Her many boyfriends are the envy of me,
She never seems to go out with one for very long
Because she is too good for them, as you can see,
Why, oh why can't she go out with me?

I have many pictures and posters of her,
Some in bikinis, some in fur,
She is always at award ceremonies and in clubs,
But I've never seen her going to the local pub.

Paris is my idol, Paris is my hero,
Without her I think I would be zero,
I wish I could meet her one day
Because there's a lot of things I would like to say.

Alex Beddard (13)
Byrchall High School

The Space Pirate

Off he went into space,
A serious look upon his face.
His mission was to fly to the sun
It would be hard but also fun.
Past the moon and past Mars
His spaceship zoomed past some stars.
After a year and a day his mission was complete,
Knowing this felt so sweet.
The sun was hot and it made him cry
So he bailed from the spaceship and fell from the sky.
Apparently he landed on the ground
But old folk say he was never found.

Jack Scott (13)
Byrchall High School

War

Tick-tock, tick-tock,
Time passes by and by,
Tick-tock, tick-tock,
Thousands of people waiting to die.

Tick-tock, tick-tock,
People running round and round,
Tick-tock, tick-tock,
The bomb is falling to the ground.

Tick-tock, tick-tock,
Jets storming through the night,
Tick-tock, tick-tock,
All the soldiers preparing to fight.

Tick-tock, tick-tock,
Britain rages on and on,
Tick-tock, tick-tock,
Hoping this war will soon be won.

Tick-tock, tick-tock,
Tick-tock, tick-tock,
Tick-tock, tick-tock
Boom!

Tick-tock, tick-tock,
All the world has gone silent,
Tick-tock, tick-tock,
But we will all remain violent.

Jason O'Keefe (13)
Byrchall High School

My World

My world is full of crazy stuff
I can't show you it's really tough
I wonder how it got there
But I really just don't care
One day I was going to bake a cake
There was a flash and I was awake.

Sean McKenna (13)
Byrchall High School

Modern And Major Historical Events

September 11th,
A pretty grim day.
To all in America,
Hoping loved ones were OK.
At 8.46 the first plane hit,
Over two-thousand died not knowing the culprit.

October 12th, 2002
While Bali was sleeping,
The nightclub grew.
The bombers took place behind the dark,
The bomb in a backpack,
Ready to kill within a spark.

December 26th, 2004
Boxing Day to people galore.
In Indonesia, a different tale,
Unknown to them a tsunami set sail.
Thousands of people clung to the trees,
While thousands more died in the seas.

July 7th, 2005
When rush-hour traffic had started to thrive.
A bus and the underground were the targets that day,
Within minutes of each other and not far away,
Fifty-two people died in London,
We then knew it was time to take action.

What is this world we live in today?
It is the world of war and dismay.
With terror and disasters happening right now
This is not what God would allow!

Katie Hillyer (13)
Byrchall High School

Childish Normality

We all want a normal life,
But is normal ever true.
Everybody is different,
Is normal me or you?

You try to blend into the crowd,
Only be noticed if you're cool.
Don't try to make yourself popular,
You will just be called a fool.

It is all because of the way you were born,
If you had brown hair or blonde,
If your eyes are green or blue,
If your hair is short or long.

If you're not as skinny as a twig,
Then there isn't a hope or chance.
You'll probably be about thirty,
When you first have romance.

But normal isn't the popular one,
It's people just like us,
People who aren't starters of trend,
People who don't make a fuss.

Louise Makin (14)
Byrchall High School

Fairy-Tale Love

Once upon a time I thought
Where does love come from?
Is it only in fairy tales?
Has all the world's love gone?

Cinderella found Prince Charming,
Each prince has found his girl,
In stories love is simple,
It's there in one quick twirl.

If you fall asleep for one hundred years,
Or get locked in a tower by your mum,
In a swish of white horses, your prince will appear
Your true love is sure to come.

Why can't love be that way in our world?
Easy to find, right in front of our eyes,
Maybe it is, you never know,
It might just be in disguise!

Laura Wood (13)
Byrchall High School

The Hedgehog

His beady eyes glare into the night
As he hears the owl hoot
Getting ready for his mission
Then off goes the light.

Cars passing by
He curls into a ball
Then lets out a whimper
As if he's to cry.

He gets ready to cross
But then he stops
A noise has approached
It could be the boss.

Its wings spread out
As it glides in the air
It releases a squawk
Almost like it's a shout.

He must stand still
Or soon he'll be prey
He looks in the distance
And there is his hill.

He stops and he freezes
And then he shoots off,
Dodging cars, dodging light
As his predator teases.

He runs in a bush
There he is safe,
He will no longer be prey
Until tomorrow's ambush.

Joanne Potter (13)
Byrchall High School

Darkness

Darkness, darkness, what is darkness?
Darkness is death, cold and dark
It comes from fear, it claws at the heart.

Whenever you are alone or when you are scared
Darkness is there, looming down
Eagerly spreading its infectious frown.

Darkness can infect the purest of minds
Corrupting the soul
Destroying all that is kind.

But even after all this evil, all this dark
There is still a salvation
Something that will save us from this eternal damnation.

For at the end of the tunnel there is always light
The creator of all that is good
It shall always shine bright.

Christopher Gannon (13)
Byrchall High School

You're Gone!

You lay there as I watch you,
You're stiff and there's no movement.
As I touch your wrist, you're cold.
There's no sign of life.

A lonely tear falls down my cheek,
I'm thinking of times we've spent together.
You and me, we were like one person,
Those times were the greatest but now they're gone.

I remember the last thing you said to me,
'Just know, I love you and always will.'
I will always know that so don't worry,
Missing you every hour of every day.

I've known you all my life,
But now you've just stepped out of it.
The funny moments settle in my head,
As reality finally hits me.

All the wonderful years with you,
Have suddenly come to a halt.
The hospital room grows lonely,
Your lively spirit already left.

In the background I hear footsteps,
Turning round as if it's you.
It's only the nurse here to turn off the machine,
I stop her as if there's a chance you could come back.

I'm stood in the corner now, too afraid,
Just staring at your lifeless body, no, I won't believe it.
The never-ending tone of the heart monitor messes with my head,
The nurse flips the switch and . . . nothing.

We're alone now, just me and you, like it used to be,
But still . . . nothing . . . you're gone.

Natalie Davies (13)
Byrchall High School

Make-Believe

We both had guns and swords with us,
Made from bananas and wooden spoons
The sofa was our pirate ship
As it sat in my old front room
The carpet underneath us
Became a shark-infested lake
And the scarf hung from the hat stand
Became a scary poisonous snake.
The chairs became small islands
With magical things to see,
An enchanted forest of mystery
Where sweets and toffee grew on every tree.
The treasure map we had
Was my mother's Woman's Weekly.
'I haven't read the problem page!'
She told us rather meekly.
Some bodies sailed along one day
And tried to take our boat,
They pounded us with knives and spears
And now our boat won't float.
'Abandon ship!' the captain cried
We swam as fast as we were able
And hid in some underground caves
Underneath the coffee table.
We played our game all day, you see
We were having such a laugh,
Pirates, treasure, boats . . . but then
Mum called us for our bath!

Vicky Murphy (14)
Byrchall High School

Lies

I'm sitting by my window,
Watching the world go by,
Making a huge effort
To keep the tear from my eye.
Why did they all lie to me?
I only want the truth.
Maybe they all think they can,
As I'm a naïve youth,
They just don't know how much it hurts,
To be deceived this way,
They all thought I'd be fine with it,
And expected me to stay.
But now my case is all packed up,
I'm leaving home tonight,
I'll wait till they're all sleeping,
And creep out at first light.
I don't know if they'll miss me,
And I don't really care,
I'm going to the city,
I should find some work there.
I never thought I'd feel this way,
I feel my heart may break,
So little do my feelings mean,
To them - so for my sake.
I have to make a fresh new start,
To begin life anew,
I must be strong and try real hard,
To see this whole thing through.

Sophie Pickles (13)
Byrchall High School

Felicity Fetlock

Felicity Fetlock was extremely horse crazy,
The love of her life was her pony called Daisy.

All night and all day she would stay in her stable,
Reading Daisy a peculiar fable.

She was eating a bag of crisps one day,
But she looked like she was munching a bale of hay.

Felicity's mother would nag, nag, nag,
'You look like you're eating out of a horse's bag!'

The poor girl got up on Friday to see
White, smelly foam lying unusually.

Her manners became extremely poor,
And she took a liking to all things raw.

She grew a mane, she grew a tail,
She slept outside in the rain and hail.

Her family said, 'Enough's enough!'
I protested but all was tough.

So Mother brought a buyer round
He bought Fliss for one hundred pounds.

Goodbye Fliss, so long, farewell,
I'll take care of Daisy, don't you dwell.

Felicity's life was now a daily slog,
Pulling a cart through mist and fog.

The lesson of this story's clear,
Consider your family and keep them near.

Emily Hughes (13)
Byrchall High School

The Universe

See in your mind's eye
The sea, the stars, the moon, the sky
Pinpricks in the vast night world
Little lights in the great abyss.

Vain little beings, we standing tall
When in reality oh, oh so small,
The sun revolves around the world
Or does the world revolve around the sun?

The moon, the sun's great reflection
Yet both are equal in retrospection,
The big cheese, the night's greatest light
But is it not also shrouded deep in darkness?

In truth the world is but a little speck
A single card in the universe's deck,
A grain of sand in the cosmic desert
And just as irritating in your eye.

Jonathan Coles (13)
Byrchall High School

Destiny

The world's ambitions have all gone.
The mysteries of the universe,
Are now unleashed upon the Earth.

But what are our ambitions now,
What do we not yet understand?
I only know of one.

Everything has been found
But there are things missing,
Things we once had.

Love and joy do not exist.
Now only war between each other is here.
Friends, family, countries torn apart.

The one I know of, no one can tell.
It changes shape, style and rhythm.
Guessing would be good, but it's useless.

Destiny is what I speak of
Forever changing direction.
Never knowing when it will end.

World peace is a thing of the past.
It was never achieved in the end.
Too many racial disagreements and wars.

We could never be united under one roof.
We could never live together,
It wouldn't work.

But perhaps if someone spoke out, against all odds.
Perhaps someone who felt their anger, their pain, their loss.
Maybe then we could live together.

Will I help them grow to love each other?
To help and support each other?
Only time and destiny will decide.

Shannon McGoldrick (13)
Byrchall High School

Upon A Star

I wish upon a star
I do it every day
I wish that I could fly
Fly, fly away from this poverty.

I wish upon a star
I do it every day
I wish that I could steer the world
Steer it away from this poverty.

I wish upon a star
I do it every day
I wish that I could run away
Away from all this poverty.

I look down from a star
I do it every day
I am going to go to Earth
To stop this poverty.

Sophie Picton (13)
Byrchall High School

At The Moss

Same time, same place
At the moss.
He left no trace
At the moss.
His fur ruffled
At the moss.
His steps muffled
At the moss.

Let off his lead
At the moss.
He ran through reeds
At the moss.
He walked so proud
At the moss.
He never barked loud
At the moss.

The rabbit bounced
At the moss.
He ran and pounced
At the moss.
The driver tried
At the moss.
But my dog died
At the moss.

Alec Stockton (13)
Byrchall High School

A Puppy's Tale

Cowering in a manky doorway
In a dark, damp and lonely street,
Crouches a bedraggled puppy dog
Matted fur a mangled mess.

A haunted look in her eyes full of fear,
Her thin body trembles if anyone nears.
Fur once so glossy, now never shines,
What was a proud bark is a strangled whine.

Lolling by her kennel
Somewhere warm and in the sun,
Lies a beautiful cocker spaniel,
No longer with any fear.

Sleek, glossy fur and a fat, full stomach,
Sparkling and heart-melting eyes.
A wagging tail that once drooped down,
Shows her happiness now a new home has been found.

Katherine Rumsey (12)
Byrchall High School

The King

Slowly, slowly, slowly,
The king prowls around his lair,
Stalking his prey,
Hunting his bounty,
Stealthfully he watches its every move
Skilfully waiting to strike
Cautiously approaching his victim.

Looking, looking, looking
So mighty and strong,
Sprinting through the grass like the wind
Darting through his wild empire,
Like royalty at its best
Marching through the land,
Conquering his world.

Walking, walking, walking
Through the jungle proudly,
Leaping from log to log with pride
Roaring with courage
And hunting with skill
Slowly, but steadily,
Completing his kill.

David Hamilton (12)
Byrchall High School

Voyage To The Stars

There was once a voyage about to set to sea
The captain and mates about to flee
To a place far, far away
But they know they're not there to stay

They're on a voyage to send poetry
To a place called Snarlox 3
This place is a very large star
You are able to see long and far

This voyage is coming to an end
They're going round the final bend
But the meaning of this voyage you see
Is to send poetry to Snarlox 3.

Jack Vickery (12)
Byrchall High School

A Thunderstorm Is . . .

A flashing light
The power of the wind
A dark cloud
Screaming people
Scary
Something which destroys everything
A horrific time
God's unhappy.

Jess Day (13)
Cansfield High School

The Sun Is . . .

A giant yellow football
A giant heater
A big yellow balloon
A big ball of fire
A massive lemon
A giant sunflower
A giant M&M
A massive sherbet lemon.

Daniel Crabtree (14)
Cansfield High School

The Sun Is . . .

A flower's food
A spaceship's view
Daylight energy
A person's suntan
A bushfire's heart
A sunflower's goal
Mosquito heaven
Swimming pool weather
A circle of fire
A world of warmth
The beginning of a new day.

Claire Pritchard (13)
Cansfield High School

Last Game At Central Park - Wigan Warriors Vs St Helens

The players walked out
To the sound of scream and shout,
Sun in the sky,
Water in the eye,
The game kicked off,
So loud you couldn't hear a cough,
Over went Betts
To the sound of a thousand jets,
The half-time whistle went,
To the air balloons we're sent.

The players came out for the last time,
Onto the pitch the colour of lime,
As the sun started to lie,
The fans began to cry,
The final whistle went,
The cheers could be heard in Kent,
The players walked round,
To the loudest sound,
Now I stand here today on Central Park Way,
And see a supermarket from after Wigan's day.

Michael Lavelle (13)
Cansfield High School

Seasons

All the seasons come and go
Winter, spring, summer and fall
Grass and trees begin to grow
Mother birds let out their call
Spring and summer go like a sprinter
Next comes fall and then winter.

The emerald leaves go golden brown
Also they go dry and crispy
Then they fall down to the ground
That the ice has made slippery
Christmas is here, winter's almost dead
But now the cycle will begin again.

Andrew Yates (13)
Cansfield High School

At Certain Times Of Year

At certain times of year
Birds sing sweetly in the trees
Everyone is full of cheer
It's so happy it brings tears
Flowers born, lambs born
My heart is simply torn.

Everyone is full of joy
The world is such a crammed place
Everywhere I look, girls, boys
Each one a different face
I'm so glad
I have a chance to be a part of that.

Hayley Evans (12)
Cansfield High School

Volcanoes

They stand proud in the mountains high
Looking down on everything around
They make horrendous echoing in the sky
With their horrible bellowing sound
They sleep for hundreds of years
The world lives in joy and fear.

The lava builds up inside
The earthquakes coming near
The other mountains start to slide
As the volcano erupts in fear
The people start to run they're scared
One might be near you, beware!

Craig Hughes (12)
Cansfield High School

The Sun, Moon And Stars

Our sun is the source of power
It stands high up in the sky
It is bigger than the Patroness tower
And it watches people that pass by.

As the night begins to fall
The sun will slip away,
And so the moon stands proud and tall
Waiting for the sun the next day.

All the stars are hanging high
And people on the ground,
The moon is floating in the sky
Waiting for the day to come around.

Chris Black (12)
Cansfield High School

Cheerful Faces

Cheerful faces, sprightly dance
The nature is a wonderful place
Underground are bustling ants
The tree bark knots like a fastened lace
A hundred daffodils at a glance
Rabbits hopping as they race
Lambs bleating as they prance
Isn't nature a wonderful thing?
It's all around us and so amazing
All these animals go back to their beds
To rest their sweet dreaming heads.

Jessica Price (12)
Cansfield High School

The Sun

As I wake up in the shining light
My eyes widen open slowly
I see such a lovely sight
I must get up sometime surely
I draw my curtains as I am lying
The sun is trying and trying.

Waving its flames around
Gazing right the way through my house
There isn't even a sound
Not even a mouse
The sun it shines just like a star
As I see it from near and far.

Toni Andrew (12)
Cansfield High School

Feather

A bird dresser
A wind presser
A pillow filler
A poet quiller
An arrow aimer
A dust tamer
A cobweb breaker
A tickle maker
A headdress sticker
A pocket pricker
Put these together
I'm a . . .

Ryan Dutton (13)
Cansfield High School

Out

Flowers spring
Leaves fall down
Bluebirds sound and sing
Owls go to town
Trees all around
Outward bound.

Sun comes out
Clouds fade away
What a doubt
Along and amongst the bay
A water downpour
Shape and claw.

Charlotte Pilling (12)
Cansfield High School

Nature

Nature has lots of different sounds
With lots of tall trees
With colours like greens and browns
And a comfortable warm breeze
Lots of birds that sing and dance
Lots of insects that prey and prance.

Nature has lots of plants
Lots of leaves on the floor
There is wildlife that dance
And a hedge shaped in a door
Lots of rivers called streams
Lots of different colourful scenes.

Robbie Smyth (13)
Cansfield High School

My Day As A Leaf

The autumn breeze wafting across my face,
I look at all the empty space where my friends used to be,
They look like a multicoloured sea.
I began to break,
The wind pulls me off my twig,
Holes come through me like burns off a cig.
I'm falling slowly and faster,
My friends cushion my fall,
It all looks like a great hall.
The wind comes, I hold on tight,
My friends struggle to fight, they let go,
I go flying.
The bus comes quick, *ouch!*
I struggle and off I go,
Up, up and up to Heaven.

Demi-Sue Roberts (11)
Cansfield High School

My Life As A Leaf

I'm enjoying the sun
And I'm having lots of fun
Peacefully in the air
Without a single care
I'm falling to the ground
And I'm making no sound
I'm as lonely as can be
Because I've fallen out of a tree
Suddenly the bell rang
Every child was kicking sand
They came over here and gave a big cheer
Ouch! They started kicking me
It was like I was out at sea
I'm turning orange and brown
And I'm making such a frown.

Lauren Woodford (11)
Cansfield High School

Stormy night

Daytime ends
And night follows,
There is gloom ahead
That is full of darkness.

Curtains drawn
As rain falls,
Splitting and crashing
While thunder roars.

Lightning striking all around
Seeking victims to be found,
Who will it find, no one knows
Shooting at random as it goes.

Josh Pearce (13)
Cansfield High School

The Breeze

I flew around as the breeze
Dancing high up in the sky
Fluttering and floating above the trees
Like a big colourful butterfly
I'd been up there for hours
Watching the beautiful flowers.

As I walked through the grass so green
It was as I remembered in my dreams
I thought of everything I'd seen
Birds and trees and fields and streams
Each one full of jumping fish
This would be my perfect wish.

Rebecca Sands (12)
Cansfield High School

Nature Down To A T

The trees are green
They hang low over land
They're beautiful to be seen
They outdo golden-yellow sand
But I've got to be fair
They're for everyone to share.

The flowers are bright
They sing a song
They go and shrink down at night
For long, so long
They're ever so fine
Even though they're not mine.

The sun shines bright
With its beaming rays
It's a beautiful sight
I could gaze and gaze
So that's nature down to a T
It is there for both you and me.

Melanie Edwards (12)
Cansfield High School

Springtime

Springtime is so much fun
Springtime the leaves are green
In spring I would like an iced bun
In a farmer's field he grows the beans
In springtime I smell the flowers
But I hate the springtime showers.

Springtime is a happy time
Springtime the apples are ripe
I love a glass of Coke and some lime
I have a water fight using the hose pipe
Springtime I go on walks
It is a good time for farmers to use pitchforks.

Jack Ross (12)
Cansfield High School

The Day And Life Of A Sun

I am the sun
Stood over the trees
Down I will come
If you say please,
Let me have tea
Then leave me be.

Thank you so much
Sorry I can't stay,
I love you such
I would have stopped
And had a play
But I had to get back up there in the sky
So everyone can see me bye, goodbye.

Kathryn Whittle (12)
Cansfield High School

Down In The Jungle

Down in the jungle, what do you see?
Have a look and see what you find.
Oh look, it's a chimpanzee, it is very kind
It is brown and looks like a clown.

Down goes the moon there is no light
Near the blue lagoon the lions fight
There are lots of bees buzzing around trees.

Ben Scott (12)
Cansfield High School

Rain

Listen to the rain
Pitter and pattering on the floor
Hear it gurgling down the drain
The rain I truly adore.
I listen to its relaxing tune
Desperately hoping it won't end soon.

Splish and splash
Down it comes,
On the floor, smash and smash
Beating like endless drums,
I listen all day
Where my mind will stray.

I listen to its song at night
And fall into deep sleep
My heart fills with great delight
For the sound of the rain in my heart it'll leap
My heart will often plea
To listen to the rain at night, oh how happy I'll be.

Kerry Charnock (12)
Cansfield High School

River

Round the river you can see
Plenty of insects and silver fishes and a big honeybee
And they watch while I do the dishes
And watch the children play
All night and day.
When the river is gushing
And the trees and bushes are blowing
And everyone is rushing and going
Because the storm is here
And it is very near.

Jamie Cook (13)
Cansfield High School

The Past Of The Failed Future

The future is dark,
The future is fear,
The future lurks above the cloud's tears!

The truth is a fright,
These wounds don't seem right,
The pain in your eyes,
Caused from all of my lies!

So many paths,
Too many roads,
My life isn't that,
But I speak out in code!

You don't look shocked
I'm not surprised!
My mouth has been locked,
And my arms are tied!

They don't understand
How scared I am!
This forgotten land
My past I have ran!

Mikki Wright (13)
Castlebrook High School

The 9/11 Experience

The boom of the bomb,
A deep growling thud of a giant's footsteps
Being engulfed in the grey grip of his hands.
The building shattering all around,
The scream of the onlookers
A high-pitched whistle as the building collapses around them.
My dreams shattered and many lives lost.

The call of the people looking for loved ones,
A bird's screech as it calls for its young,
Many, many high-pitched screeches
Shattering a beautiful world.
The ripple of the flag in the wind,
An eagle standing on top of the world proudly, wings billowing.

As the shadow of a plane is reflected, it crashes,
An angry lion's roar as it starts to shatter,
The skyscraper, a long, large book full of wonders starts to melt.

Jennifer Butler (13)
Castlebrook High School

A Sting Of Pain

Wasps are horrid, vicious and bad,
When stung it was the worst pain I've had.
Yellow and black with a great big sting,
Who invented this nasty thing?
Drunk in the autumn on rotting fruit,
Looking for trouble, I just want to shoot.
When I hear the buzzing, I feel nothing but fear,
I run as fast as I can, I don't want it near.
My nightmare begins when I hear that noise,
It's the only thing that makes me annoyed!

Elizabeth Mitchell (13)
Castlebrook High School

The Youngest Darkness

Here I am all alone,
Sitting here on my own,
Nothing here and nothing there,
Alone, just on my own.

What's this I see?
Getting closer and closer to me,
I think it's a vehicle,
His favourite choice.

One to my left and one to my right,
But still only just in my sight.

Hey, what's this, can it be?
Another form of the ones chasing me?
I climb on the top
And the fear that was, starts to stop.

Wait, no, not again,
It's some kind of train,
It's danger once again,
I think it's my time!

One to my left and one to my right,
But still only just in my sight.

I might have been wrong,
But I jumped off the side,
I feel safe once again,
But for just how long?

I shouldn't be so sure,
But yet I am still here,
Two wheels of death,
Two of him coming near.

One to my left and one to my right,
But still only just in my sight.

I go back on top hoping it'll stop,
Yet another mistake,
So the six that had gone
Brought me to wake.

Daniel Whatmough (13)
Castlebrook High School

Doom In The Forest

Bears do not deserve their reputation
They are the Devil's assassin,
In an innocent disguise,
They are evil.

They live in the forest,
It is a trap,
Luring innocent people to their death,
Just like the Gates of Hell.

The moon sees it all,
It belongs to the Grim Reaper,
It is his searchlight,
Bringing death.

Night begins it,
It is the wake up call
For death
No one can survive it.

The dark spreads,
Bringing its purpose,
It is the end,
The end of everything.

All this,
Spells out one thing,
It spells
Doom.

But one way remains
Light,
It is the saviour,
A misguided tale.

David Meehan (13)
Castlebrook High School

The Unknown Path

A long dark corridor is a distant future,
You'll never know if it will suit you,
A blindfold is a big black monster,
You'll be afraid it will hurt you,
A murderer is life's true ending,
In no time he will be spending,
A grave is your last sleeping place,
Never again will you tie your lace,
A tied rope is a barrier of freedom,
Until someone comes and then they free them,
You may be killed with a knife,
So I suggest you enjoy your life.

Peter Harris (13)
Castlebrook High School

The Demon Dentist

The dentist is the son of Satan
I walk along the cursed room
And sit in the cursed chair
Oh Lord, my Lord help me.

He whispers, 'Open wide'
I open up with fear
His tools go in
His mouth begins to grin
Four teeth will be on their way.

Oh no, I start to scream
The pain will be demonic
I hate this man, this evil man
Or maybe it's a girl?

Tom Connolly (14)
Castlebrook High School

Beautifully Broken

Our fears that we cage deep inside our souls,
The penetrating eyes that peer from the holes,
Cold shivers that race down our spine,
One quick pounce and now you're mine.

The skies darken and the wind roars,
Scrambling over my body and surrounding the floor,
As I start to tremble and wait my fate,
My poisoned heart brews with hate.

Death's evil blanket suffocates me,
I'm slowly dying, can't you see?
They scar me those knives and spears,
My eyes drowning in my stolen fears.

Shut your eyes and drift away,
Those evil creatures I shall face one day,
The curse for the worst, live to kill,
From snatching lives a kick, a thrill.

I'm beautiful broken, lost in my youth,
I keep locked inside me the hate and the truth,
My memories lost in the rain like tears,
They wipe away my pain and fears.

Charlotte McDonald (13)
Castlebrook High School

Haunting Fears

Fear is a monster that swallows you whole
My fear is a world living alone
Loneliness is a nightmare you can't run from
Filling your throat with shattered glass
Like the hearts of your loved ones
Broken and smashed

Loneliness forwards you to search for someone
But each house you pass no one is home
No door unlocked welcoming friends
No streaming light inviting you in
All warmth and kindness hidden within

Filling my life is death itself
As black and haunting as the Grim Reaper himself
Attacking your family and friends at will
Leaving you lonely lost in a place
A nailed shut box closing in on loved ones
Above a slab of stone carved with no care or grace

Now all that's left to say is that
This is my nightmare
That is the truth
This is the fear
Haunting my youth.

Amy Fielder (13)
Castlebrook High School

Tiger's Prey

My nightmare scream is entering death
Which is the dark hole of the tiger's stomach.
The freefall plummet down the tiger's throat entering my final sleep.
We stood alone in the dark deserted forest
My final moments lie before me, breathe again, I shall not.

Fear is travelling down my body, through my blood.
When will I wake up, this has to be a dream.
The tiger licks his lips, ready, prepared for the kill,
Soon I am finished, that will be that.

He's faster, smarter and much more agile,
And soon I am his prey, his food for a week.
My fears have come true; I now enter his sight,
The tiger's roar is the beginning of the end!

The creature's tooth which is that razor blade,
Is soon to be used as a horrific weapon.
He opens his mouth; I can see it coming,
And there it is . . .

Dominic Comrie (14)
Castlebrook High School

Overcoming Fears

An ambulance is a one-way ticket to Hell
Stepping into the blood-stained gates
The spikes strike fear
All because I broke my leg.

Lying down in a boring, lonely pit
The beds are lumpy
The food's disgusting
All because I broke my leg.

The operation was so painful
The painkillers are not working
The pain is unbearable
All because I broke my leg.

Finally I get the all clear
I step into freedom
It feels fantastic
All because I broke my leg.

Physiotherapy, sudden pains, check-ups
I'm back
Facing my fear
All because I broke my leg.

It's all over
I'm as fit as a fiddle
I'm recovered
All because I broke my leg.

I feel so sick
I can't even walk
I can't go back
All because I broke my leg.

I'm here
But I'm not scared
I've beaten it
My fear has gone
All because I broke my leg.

Lewis Thelwell (13)
Castlebrook High School

Fear

A prison cell is isolation from the outside world
Certainly no place for an innocent girl
Loneliness is like a padlocked door
Where nothing is certain, nothing is sure
Uncertainty is being dumped at a crossroads
Not knowing which way to choose
Like a devil's game,
He leaves you confused
A coffin is a death sentence
Life is a blur and nothing makes sense
Hiding, hiding away from the sun
Living in shadows will never be fun
Life is a challenge, a test set by angels
Winning is joyful, one mistake and you lose.

Danielle Leigh (14)
Castlebrook High School

Killer Canines

Vicious dogs are the wolves of the city
They are much more dangerous than a cute kitty
The owners use them for their reputation
They're more brutal than those at the police station.

'Their bark is worse than their bite,' say the owners, that's not true
I'm sure those beasts can kill you!
The thought of their carnivorous teeth breaking my skin
Could only be a punishment for my greatest sin.

I can see them at the end of Satan's lead
Panting, waiting for their next feed
Once bitten, twice is shy
My fear eats me up, I cannot lie.

I dread the day I'll meet it again
I wear thick clothes to ease the pain
It senses my terror and clenches its jaw
Someone help! I can't take it anymore.

Kamo Kupi (14)
Castlebrook High School

Drops Into Depression

My nightmare scream
Is a drop into a river
That swallows me
Into a swirling black hole!

The long river is ink
From a leaking fountain!

My heart beats
Like African dancers!

I long to see the sun
In my eyes, feel its heat
Not in my mind!

A skyscraper is a block
Of tumbling Lego
That a child pushes by!

Laura Clough (13)
Castlebrook High School

Falling

Bees don't deserve the freedom of our air,
With their eyes of evil glaring as you stare,
The Devil's pets which patrol our skies
Are piercing and tormenting all things that don't fly.

I'm swaying at the peak of a floodlit structure,
Dangling over the edge glaring at the floor,
With Satan's henchmen knocking at my door
With the Gates of Heaven drifting by.

As I plunge down with no harness,
It becomes hard to imagine the good things,
Slowly my body turns to stone,
With my lifeless carcass plummeting to the last black hole.

Despair is what my family feels,
As they watch powerless in my final journey
Tears are shed, all hope is lost.

Andrew Gregoriou (13)
Castlebrook High School

Nightmare Scream

So many answers, so little time,
Who are these creatures we fear inside?
People think leeches are sent to steal our blood,
Or are they simply misunderstood?
Spiders are eight eyes watching you all the time,
Ready to pounce at you if you step out of line.
Is death a blessing or a curse?
Most people think there's nothing worse.
Is death God's way of saying you're fired?
Your number's up, it's time to go,
We'll see you very soon you know.
Death could just be a final sleep,
It doesn't hurt, there's no need to weep.
I don't mean to worry you as it's rather mean,
But you'll be very lucky to survive a nightmare scream!

Jessica Endacott (14)
Castlebrook High School

The Truth Of Spiders

The spider is a ball of spiky hell,
They come out at night to haunt you.
They are the Grim Reaper of the spiders coming to torture you,
Their small beady eyes filled with pure hatred.

Their teeny bodies,
Their fat, long legs,
Beady eyes and heart of stone.

The blackness of their furry body is a shadow of broken dreams,
Their darkness is a place of flying daggers.
They are humans' worst enemy
But what are we to do?

Paige Edwards (13)
Castlebrook High School

The Spell Of Darkness

The woods are sinking into a black lagoon of never-ending fears,
The sun has been washed away with my screaming tears.
I let out a piercing shriek and cry,
As I see the trees' branches reach up to the sky.

Clawing out the sparkling stars
Out from the darkness near and far.
A shadow quickly flickers past,
But I don't know why it went so fast.

A shiver rushes down my spine,
A moment suddenly freezes in time.
My heart stops, as my mouth drops.

I notice a spider sent from Hell,
Is emerging from the underworld to cast his evil spell.
A quick blast of smoke and it all goes blank,
Now I know that death is a black hole of nothingness.

Emma Birtles (13)
Castlebrook High School

The Nature Of Evil

The gates to your future are dark and dead,
The angels that were protecting, all have fled,
Satan's right hand man is grim,
Your afterlife becomes a giant sin,
The moonlight stalker stalks his prey,
Then prepares to make his slay,
The fog of death swallowing your life,
Disguising itself as a kitchen knife,
The moonlight stalker with his killing machines,
His eyeballs suffocating with glaring beams,
There's a torchlight shining in the dark,
Listen to the herald angels hark,
Heaven shining in the sky,
That is where you really lie,
From Hell to Heaven you have been hurled,
Let's prepare for the end of the world.

Andrew Garner (14)
Castlebrook High School

My Nightmare Scream - Nuclear Holocaust

Bang!
Bang!
The man falls taking the world with him.
The planet withers.
Bush is dead.

The world is shocked.
Appalled.
America drops its payload.
Nuclear bombs.

One of the first,
Is showcased as a hero,
Yet he is a murderer.
He is the fat man.

Trinity
The very first.
A boil of cruel death.
In the desert
All life is killed in an instant,
As trinity goes boom.

Operation hurricane,
Our experiment.
They blew up a ship.
Left a 350m wide crater it did.
No kidding.

Little boy,
Rather harmless.
But don't drop it.
Hiroshima never stood a chance.

Chernobyl
A nuclear plant.
It went *boom!*
In Russia it did.
But we got acid rain here.

Badger
A common animal
With a thief's mask
But in America it has a killer's mask
A giant mushroom killed.

America.
Will it seal its borders?
Declare war on the world
Hit Russia's share of bombs
Wipe out the world.
Kill itself in the process?

And Mr Bush
Knowing that if he goes down,
The world will go with him.
Not good for the ego.
No good for the world.

He can do anything
And get away with it.
If he weren't American
He would be a war criminal.

He could rule in a Zimmer frame.
Be preserved in a cryogenic chamber.
Be a disembodied head
Just saying . . .
'Invade X.'

What would the world do?
The UN would be powerless
In the face of world decimation.

What fate befalls us?

Henry Hudnott (13)
Castlebrook High School

My Nightmare Scream Poem - The Nightmare Of Being Buried

Rats are an accident waiting to happen,
I wish someone would just flatten them.
Being buried is the final sleep,
But for the rats it's like having a Christmas feast.
They are as fast as lightning,
And extremely frightening.
Rats are the Devil's best friend,
Whilst you're buried they nibble at you but there's no time to mend.
Rats are scruffy balls of fluff,
Under your grave it's hard to be rough and tough.
Rats are smaller versions of tigers,
Ten times worse than spiders.
So that's my nightmare dream,
Or should I say nightmare scream!

Abbi Davies (14)
Castlebrook High School

Something Strange

I saw a box with big brown branches moving with a hint of rhythm.
I saw a tree with orange hair swaying in the midday air.
I saw a book with devil eyes soaring through the cover.
I saw a lion with yellow fangs looking like bananas.
I saw a cat gliding through the sky with monstrous wings
And then I saw a bird looking down on me wondering what I could see!

Jessica Szpak (13)
Castlebrook High School

My Mixed-Up Dream

I saw a rabbit riding a grey pony in my bedroom.
I saw a well walking on the blue sea in a small village.
I saw a dog with royal blue water inside floating up and down.
I saw a bear with short white fur running rapidly.
I saw a horse rider with short brown fur that was shining.
I saw a blanket in the middle of a hot rainforest.

Emily Owen (12)
Castlebrook High School

Animal Land

I saw a goat flying in the sky with purple skin and gold eyes.
I saw a football reading a book.
I saw a pig trimming his long purple beard.
I saw a donkey with red and pink fur.
I saw a tiger flying through the air.
I saw a cow sledging in the sea.

James Wharmby (12)
Castlebrook High School

A Poem About A Footballer

The whistle blows, the game is on.
It comes to his feet but the ball has soon gone.

He's down the pitch raring for goal.
He shoots, he scores, all the crowd roars.

The ref blows for centre, he's in black and white.
He blows the whistle, it's time to fight.

He passes backwards then crosses the ball.
He looks for the person who's very tall.

He leaps up high and heads it just wide.
The linesman flags as he was offside.

The game is not over, there's one minute to go.
Both teams start shouting for that winning goal.

The corner comes in, he volleys in the net.
The keeper's downhearted and could lose his bet.

At last the sound they all want to hear.
The crowd jumps up and gives a big cheer.

The game is now over, the fans leave the ground.
Everyone's gone home and now there's no sound.

Michael Cafferkey (11)
Hutton Grammar School

The Footballer

He hit the ball
As the player dived to tackle him.
He jumped out of the way while they slid towards him.
The wet ground let him pass smoothly.
The crowd roared
As the ball struck the back of the net.
The whistle blew to restart the match.
The opposition lofted the ball over the defence.
The keeper smothered the ball,
He kicked it into the sky.
He jumped up and headed it on.
It was a nail biting moment as the striker placed it back
He took it past them.
He used stopovers and tricks like you've never seen.
The crowd screamed as the ball pinged off the cross-bar!
The moment came when the ref blew the whistle.
They went and celebrated, the atmosphere was magic.
The cup had been won, he was a hero.

Mark Gowdy (11)
Hutton Grammar School

The Rollerblader

The wheels are turning rapidly,
Building speed up to the ramp.
He jumps onto the grind bar,
Sliding at the speed of light.
He's made it, the crowd cheers,
As he rolls back to the half pipe.
He stops suddenly,
No one has ever completed it without falling off.
Can he do it?
The gun sounds,
He is off.
As he rolls in it all goes silent,
The crowd waits patiently.
Then he comes shooting out of the end,
He has done it.
The first person ever
But how long will it last?

Ashley Clitheroe (11)
Hutton Grammar School

The Tennis Player

If the ball ever came close to my racquet
Since I was a boy I would just go to whack it!
It has been my dream since I was a boy
To have a racquet in my hand.
With the crowd going wild
My rival gracious in defeat,
And I am clutching the title.
Wimbledon, my first Grand Slam.
But will it always be a dream?
Who knows?
I will just keep practising until this is a reality,
This is my dream; I want to make it come true.

William Powley (11)
Hutton Grammar School

The Same Old Story

A gentle misty rain
Softly caresses
The bodies of
An endless
And stationary
Line of sober coloured
Saloons and
Gas-guzzling people carriers,
Also sober, like most of the occupants.

8.27. Five minutes more.
Another song on the radio.
Another five feet forward.
The rain presses
A little deeper,
Until it impresses upon
The minds of
The defeated chauffeurs,
Their bleary-eyed passengers
Gazing morosely on.

Another four feet forward.
The dumping spots
Are scarcely closer.
Infant passengers stamp and howl,
Premeditating
The waiting gale.

A jingle on the radio.
A jingle from a taunting cyclist's bell.
Coming through, they cry
Ignoring the irony
And the rain.
Radio off.
A jingle is no place
For a sober car.

Another five minutes,
Another five feet forward.

Andy Irwin (17)
Hutton Grammar School

The Basketball Player

This is a poem about a player of basketball,
One team wins, the another has to fall.
The whistle blows and the game is now on,
The competition and dedication is second to none.
The referee dressed in white and black,
The player takes a shot, *smack!*

The backboard wobbles as does the ball,
The player jumps but does not want to fall,
The friction of the trainers makes a screech,
He goes for a slam dunk but cannot reach.
In the last two seconds a team scores,
Excitedly the crowd roars,
That team runs off to celebrate,
As the opposition dawdle off in dismay.

Philip Burns (11)
Hutton Grammar School

Flying Away

On the stairs I sat
Listening to their latest spat
Tears flowing from my face
My family in disgrace.

All I can hear is the anger and rage
Feeling like I am trapped in a cage
Hoping things would be OK
I just wanted to see the light of day.

Years, years we have waited
For this subject to be debated
Whether or not we stay or go
Neither she nor I do know.

All I want is to be carefree
Not to worry about my whole family
Time and time again I dream of it
A life where my family is completely split.

One day I sit and listen to her
Telling me how it isn't fair
But we have to leave and start afresh
As she says this, colour drains from my flesh.

So now I must face my greatest fear
To hold my family year after year
While we sit in our rented flat
Not even able to afford a front doormat.

But away from the arguments and tears
I may be able to conquer my fears,
Of flying away from the unknown
Finding somewhere new I can call home.

Sam Rigby (15)
Hutton Grammar School

The Greatest Golfer

Whoosh goes the club, wood or iron
As he hits the ball and sends it flyin'
He might hear a splash as it lands in the lake
Then he will say, 'For goodness sake!'
The hole's very long, the ball is hit wide
Straight into the bunker that lies on the side.
He turns to his caddie and begins to talk
While they set off together on their tiring walk.
Now in the bunker his efforts doubled
With the sand rising as his anger bubbled.
Once on the green he produces his putter
That creates a shot to make the crowd splutter.
He'd like to get the top prize with a hole in one
But on this current form that wish is soon gone.
He's been round the world to all the big games
Now back at home he can't remember the names.
Palm Springs, Gleneagles, Woods and Montgomery
They now merge together in one hazy memory.
He reaches the clubhouse and looks behind
The world's greatest golfer, all in his mind.

Peter Tipping (11)
Hutton Grammar School

Being In Care

They say there is a reason,
They say they don't have a choice,
But I still sit there begging
They just ignore my voice.
People see what's on the outside
But it's on the inside that counts,
I lie in bed alone every night
And cry my heart out.
I wish I could go home
But I feel I'm on my own, all alone.
I have no one to speak to
What have I done to you?
I lived somewhere, I was happy
But I still get moved because of money.
Sometimes I think my life is a mistake
Because look at it, it's all fake!
If I could prove to people what I've been through
They wouldn't believe it because it sounds untrue!

Jodie Parker (15)
Larches House Hostel School

My Shopping Poem

I love to spend the weekend shopping for new clothes,
New things for me to wear from my head down to my toes.
I love Gucci, Prada, Dolce and Gabbana!

Heels and platforms are the best shoes,
Pumps and trainers give me the blues.
I like to stand tall, above the rest,
My Louis Vuitton's are by far the best.

Necklaces, bracelets, earrings, bangles,
I like jewellery that glitters and dangles.
Toe rings and anklelets are my favourite too,
I love shopping; it's what I like to do!

Alex Leigh (11)
Little Lever School Specialist Language College

Tennis

June is bursting out all over,
The Wimbledon courts are cleared of their clover.
Each player hoping for game, set and match,
The umpire above in his own little patch.
Spectators arriving to courts one, two and three,
Vendors selling strawberry and cream tea.
Ballboys waiting in anticipation,
Quietly enjoying their relaxation.
The players arriving loaded with gear,
And all the spectators given a rousing cheer.
At last it is time for the game to commence
And everybody's ready for this major event.
Winner or loser what will he be,
The sets are already 6-4, 6-3.
Now he is a Grand Slam winner
He's looking forward to a celebratory dinner.

Cole Bradley (11)
Little Lever School Specialist Language College

Dreams

Dreams, what are they?
Another life when we are asleep.
Sometimes making you laugh in the night
Or cry out with fear.

Nobody knows when they fall asleep
What will happen to them.
Will it be a dream come true
Or a nasty nightmare?

Scary dreams, sweet dreams,
Funny dreams or sad dreams.
Monsters chasing, chocolate factories.
Circus clowns or someone crying.
Dreams, what are they?

Aylish Doherty (11)
Little Lever School Specialist Language College

Winter

Winter never fails to surprise
With snow and hail
Wind and rain.

We play in the snow
Making snowmen
Having snow fights.

Hats, gloves, scarves
Keep our bodies warm
Toes going blue
Noses going red.

Frosty blankets covering your lawns
Snowflakes on your eyelashes
Ice on your cars
You never know which one or all will come.

One thing that's for certain is
Whatever the weather
Winter has Christmas
For that I adore it.

Laura Hinchliffe (14)
Little Lever School Specialist Language College

Love Of A Teenage Girl

Every day is a struggle
Thoughts rushing through my mind.
What to wear? How to look?
All I seem to think about is boys, boys and more boys.
But when you find that special someone
Your heart stops, you start blushing.
And that's how I knew.
People say there's no such thing as love at fifteen.
What would they know?
I feel passionately about a special someone,
They all think I've gone crazy.
Love isn't something people can tamper with,
It's a very strong unusual feeling.
When you fall in love you will understand.

Hannah Wallwork (14)
Little Lever School Specialist Language College

Performing Pressure

I was struck by the blinding overhead lights.
Beads of sweat trickled down my forehead and my heart almost leaped
out of my chest,
Pounding inside me like a wild animal fighting to escape its cage.
I stumbled around to find my feet and stand correctly in my position.
I could almost feel sharp pains inside me
Caused by the audience and their piercing stares.
Each and every one of them, all like pin-pricks in the distance.
My stomach was almost crushed, as it suddenly felt as if it had hit the
ground.
My body quivering, adrenalin pumping through my every limb,
I performed my act triumphantly, acting like there was no tomorrow.
The crowd roared and were applauding me as my act came to an
amazing end.
A huge weight had been lifted from me and I felt more confident,
Much more confident than I had felt in all my life.

Rebecca Marsden (14)
Little Lever School Specialist Language College

Someone Special

When you meet that special person,
And they give you that smile,
You get all hot and bothered
And the world just seems to stop,
Or you can't concentrate on anything,
You can't even talk,
But then you pull yourself together and just smile back.

Nadia Bourka (14)
Little Lever School Specialist Language College

Body

He stands over the body, covered in blood,
The body lies bruised from the struggle,
Just an innocent girl taken by a cruel man.
The wind outside howls through the doorframe.
Black sheets covering the windows, blocking out life.
The darkness of the room shudders through the body,
The murderer moves back facing his crime,
Just an hour ago walking round, now helplessly on the ground.

Nicole Darbyshire (14)
Little Lever School Specialist Language College

Sox

The stray cat wandered in curiously
Looking around in anticipation.
We called her Sox because she has white paws.
Her green eyes glistening as she looks up
At us, obviously begging for some milk.
She purrs softly as she brushes against
Our bare legs before lazing in the sun.
Her tail swiftly stirring as she moves her
Silky whiskers on her tabby coloured head.

Jennie Carter (14)
Little Lever School Specialist Language College

All About Me!

My name is Hannah; I'm eleven years old,
I'm small and cute, or so I'm told!
In my house there is one mum
There is also a cat that weighs a tonne,
There are three girls, like three wise men,
Sometimes it feels like there are ten.

The noise is deafening from day to day,
The girls and Mum all want their say,
Time together we try to make,
We play a game or bake a cake.

We all settle down after dark,
After games at home and time in the park,
Mum and me, we have a cuddle,
And tomorrow brings another muddle!

Hannah Westwood (11)
Little Lever School Specialist Language College

Designer Names

Gucci, Prada, Dolce & Gabbana, so many names to choose.
Not just names but the language of love spoken by style gurus.

Calvin Klein, Louis Vuitton, Monsieur Yves Saint Laurent
Are the men women want in their lives.
When you've felt the caress of a Versace dress, the others you'll learn
to despise.

You can learn to forget, that cheap eau de toilette
You'll need some expensive French perfume
To give your presence that va, va, voom!

So go out to the store and get yourself some real haute couture
Buy just as much as you desire before your credit card expires!

Elyse Taylor (12)
Little Lever School Specialist Language College

I Just Can't Stand . . .

I just can't stand . . .
The way liver has to sliver.
Why kidney has to rhyme with Sidney.
The way tomatoes look like my toes.
The way pickle makes me tickle.
The way cucumber has to hum.
The way rice makes me dice.
The way cod makes me have a big thud.
The way the poem has to end.

Jade Harrison (13)
Little Lever School Specialist Language College

Autumn Poem

Red, gold, orange and brown,
Leaves are scattered on the ground,
Days are shorter, night comes quicker,
Trees are bare and mist is thicker.

Barbecue is packed away,
Too cold to eat outside these days,
Too wet for football, too cold to play,
Better get out my Xbox today.

Cars with headlights, street lights on,
Where has all the nice weather gone?
The weather report suggests a hat and scarf,
Because the temperature has dropped by half.

Extra covers on my bed,
Pulled up close around my head,
I feel the cold, I wish it was warmer
But Bonfire Night's just around the corner.

Connor Peploe (12)
Little Lever School Specialist Language College

Eyes Wide Open

Dominican Republic here I come
Suitcase packed full of designer gear
Exotic holidays, ideal scenery
Greeted by a hot gush of air
So humid I couldn't breathe.

Marengue playing cultural tunes
'Tips, tips, tips, welcome.'

Along the open road we go
A culture shock I get
Shanty towns as far as the eye can see
Feeling all confused!

'Tips, tips, tips!'

Along the roadside young children stand
Like dogs begging for food
Their hands outstretched
Young, starving faces looking at you.

'Tips, tips, tips!'

Big houses posh cars, iPods
What have they got?
All that I see is their faces,
They have nothing but still smile, sing and dance!

I will never take anything for granted again!

Aimee Fishwick (14)
Little Lever School Specialist Language College

Autumn Leaves

The blazing heat of summer has past
Now autumn brings a breezy blast.
With colours of yellow, orange and golden brown
The leaves come tumbling to the ground.

Whilst the leaves are falling
And I am outside walking.
I hear a brittle crunching sound
As I tread them to the ground.

After school it soon goes dark
And the junkyard dog gives a bark.
As on children's faces are cheeky smiles
When they've kicked over fresh swept piles.

So off to bed with teddy I take
Then in the morning I awake.
All day long the teachers taught a sum,
This is what we all call autumn.

Chelsey Raby (13)
Little Lever School Specialist Language College

Autumn Fairies

Riding leaves like a horse
As they float to the ground
All the leaves on the floor
And all the fairies dancing round.

All the fairies sing and sing
'Bout all the autumn things
Colours, leaves and shedding trees
And especially the autumn breeze.

Autumn is ending, it's nearly winter
The fairies try not to shed a tear
So they all go and hibernate
And wait for the autumn next year.

Natasha Jamieson (12)
Little Lever School Specialist Language College

If I Could Go Anywhere

If I could go anywhere
I would go up in space.
The aliens and spaceships,
Wow! Cool! But way up there.

If I could go anywhere
I'd go trailing in the jungle.
The tigers and the monkeys
All hiding somewhere.

If I could go anywhere
I'd go to the North Pole.
Polar bears and Eskimos,
But what do you wear?

If I would be anywhere
I would be right here.
The tree and the presents,
Christmas is near!

Lauren Roberts (15)
Little Lever School Specialist Language College

Autumn, Oh Autumn

Autumn, oh autumn,
What a beautiful season,
So good, you don't need a reason.

Autumn, oh autumn,
There are lots of different leaves,
Lots of different colours,
And lots of bare trees.

Autumn, oh autumn,
What a beautiful season
And there can only be one reason.

The reason is that you make me smile,
Even though, it's only for a while,
All I can say is
I can't wait till I see you again!

Autumn, oh wonderful autumn,
The leaves are all blowing away,
Why can't you stay?

Rebecca Gent (13)
Little Lever School Specialist Language College

Being Famous

Being famous must be hard,
Everything you do, say,
Even the things you don't want people to know,
Is printed in every paper,
But even with all this publicity,
It must be fun.
Being in movies,
Your name known by everyone,
Plus, you make us laugh,
We love you and your work
You can sing, dance and ct,
But most of all you make us feel different
And you become our idols
Till the next star comes along!

Jessica Baird (13)
Little Lever School Specialist Language College

Autumn

In autumn the crispy, crunchy leaves are gathered and burnt by the gardeners.
In autumn the bare trees fall into their autumn sleep.
In autumn the squirrels forage for acorns and berries.
In autumn the misty mornings, roll slowly into the short days.
In autumn we stand on the playground and play with the conkers we've collected.
In autumn the leaves turn from green to gold, crimson, orange, brown, yellow and red.
In autumn the days get shorter as the clocks get turned back.
In autumn the birds migrate and we hibernate.

Sarah Gee (14)
Little Lever School Specialist Language College

Cricket Poem

The ball is released out of the bowler's hand.
The batsmen watches where the ball will land.
The batsman gets ready to play the drive.
He looks at mid-off seeing if he'll survive.
The ball connects and one bounce four,
The crowd are shouting, 'Give us more.'
The batsman looks for how much is needed,
The non-strikers say, 'Don't worry, you've succeeded.'

Sajjad Pervez (11)
Little Lever School Specialist Language College

Melissa

You've always been there from the start,
For this I love you with all my heart.
Sometimes you act the clown,
But always tell when I'm down.
Together we've had giggles and tears,
Shared and faced our deepest fears.
We have our differences, clothes and boys
But unlike many, we don't play with toys.
We'll always share those special days,
The ones I treasure, I cannot say,
You've been there for me through thick and thin,
I look back and grin.

Kaya Smith (13)
Little Lever School Specialist Language College

Autumn Days

In autumn when trees are brown,
The tiny leaves come tumbling down,
They don't make the slightest sound
But lie so quietly on the ground
Until the wind comes huffing by,
It blows them off towards the sky.

Rebecca Rothwell (13)
Little Lever School Specialist Language College

Heaven

Some say the grass is greener on the other side but not in this place.
Above all the towns and cities you can see a place
Free from war and destruction, where no hand has touched and no
man has gone.
In this place there are no outcasts, no laws or systems.
There is peace, food and love.
The birds sing and the trees sway.
There is no government or pollution, people do and say as they please.
Above the clouds this place is on a mountain
Made of gold and a throne for every man's soul.

Axl Thomas (13)
Little Lever School Specialist Language College

Trip

The letters come, about time too,
After six weeks wait, you got a place.
You're running, screaming through the house.
Already planning what to wear,
Wonder if you're scared of flying.

Arrangements confusing, but the day rolls around,
You stand with your suitcase on the train platform.
Your mother's getting tearful,
Her little girl's first trip abroad!
She always forgets you're fifteen, not three!

The train's late, by half an hour at least.
You're not too sure; your watch is set to German time.
The sky is clear but it's freezing cold.
It'll be worse over there, wrap up warm they told you,
You're the only one who remembered.

Who knew airports could be so much fun?
Go down the up escalator and fall flat on your face.
Girls run amok in the off-licence and boys sit looking bored.
There's a competition for who's got the heaviest luggage,
You come somewhere in the middle.

The plane's smaller than you thought, you're disappointed.
You get the window seat, the right-hand aisle.
Your friend is fretting about a fear of heights,
As well as claustrophobia and travel sickness.
You give her your paper bag.

The crawl up the runway is agonisingly slow.
You're sick of the air hostess already.
The take-off's fantastic, you love it.
Your friend turns, hesitates, opens her mouth,
'Can we do it again?'

Jennifer Mort (15)
Little Lever School Specialist Language College

My Poem About A Tiger

The look in their eyes.
The fear in their eyes.
The hatred in their eyes.
The sharpness of the teeth.
The redness of the teeth.
The size of the teeth.
The pain of the prey.
The joyfulness of the predator.
The silence of death
And the loudness of the killing.

Mark Chodacki (13)
Little Lever School Specialist Language College

Where To Live?

I wonder where to live.
There is Germany but they don't like the English
Or maybe even France but I can't speak French.
I wonder where to live.
I know New Zealand, but what about my family
They said they wanted to go to India,
But I don't like India as it is so dull.
America is a nice place but it is too expensive.
I just don't know where to live.
Maybe Spain, maybe Italy.
No, I have been there.
I want to go to a new place.
I have finally got it
Australia, sun, sea, it's got everything I need.

Luke Brown (13)
Lostock Hall Community High School

The Tomb

Life has become so big now
It's like you're stuck in a gigantic room
I asked myself why and how
All I know is that I'm trapped in a tomb.

My life flashed before my eyes
I shout out that I am here
No one heard, I'm gonna die
So I sit, life slipping away fearfully.

I thought there must be a way
All I know is I'm stuck in Hell
Who kidnapped me is gonna pay
If I get out I'm going to tell.

People I know because I will be down
I finally get found, I go home to Strand
People ask me in town
But all I say is that you won't understand.

Phillip Cook (13)
Lostock Hall Community High School

Stop Racism

Why are we so bothered about other people's race,
Their personal appearance, the look on their face?
We shouldn't be bothered if we are black or white
As long as we all know what's wrong from right.
We shouldn't insult or discriminate their beliefs
I'd love to hear the huge sigh of relief
From telling them there will be no racism,
No bullying, no sexism.
If we ever stop all the racist arguments and riots
The world would be a lot more peaceful and quiet.

Amy Finch (13)
Lostock Hall Community High School

Hopes, Dreams And Ambitions

I have a dream to live in a world were people are all equal as each
other.
I have a hope that people will accept me for who I am,
Not my looks but who's the real me.
I have a destiny to be who I want to be,
Forget blacks and whites or who's wrong and right.
Working as a team is what I believe in.
Friendship, partnership are what you really need.
It's the key to life you know, having one of you and me.
I have a dream to travel to Mars, meet new friends and to be like a star.
I have a hope to join the armed forces, get into distraught situations,
That's what I live for.
I have a danger deep inside me, the danger and anger that gets me
into trouble.
Danger is the devil inside me, the one that gets me grounded.
I wish I had a loving mum and dad, who would treat me like royalty,
But what I wish for and what I get are two different things.
I wish I was dead, buried deep within the ground.
I wish I lay buried next to my mum and be happy as can be.
I have a dream; all I really want to be is me!

Sara-Louise Kelly (13)
Lostock Hall Community High School

The Cold Weather

I am shivering standing alone
The cavern engulfs me
I can see an icicle
It's glimmering in my eye.

I can feel the frost cold
Sitting in the palm of my hand
I can hear a crunch and
A rich crisp noise.

I can see and hear
Water trickling into a silver stream.

Abbie Dawson (13)
Lostock Hall Community High School

The War

Bullets going this way and that,
Soldiers dying in their bunkers,
Germans bombing us,
Britain bombing them.
Oh I wish I was at home.

The regrets I feel
For lying about my age,
This bunker is like a huge cage,
Oh I wish I was at home.

My friend taking a bullet to his head,
Oh, I want those Germans dead.
My anger takes it out on them,
Oh I wish I was at home.

More and more bodies were going down,
My facial expression starts to frown,
Oh I wish I was at home.

Finally when the war had ended,
The bodies started to get older,
There was me in the mud,
In my head was a silver stud,
Oh I wish I was at home.

Josh Blakeston (13)
Lostock Hall Community High School

Hallowe'en Tiara

'My tiara is so not,'
I heard my best friend say
We are having a Hallowe'en party by the way.

As I flicked on the radio
It was a Hallowe'en special
It was on DJ Rankin though.

This brought on a feeling of pure fear
This brought on a feeling of fright through the night.

All of us screamed as my brother sneaked in on us
Both of my brothers did it
It was one or the other.

We laughed our heads off
As my brother's face lit up
As we all went to bed
I still have my tiara upon my head!

Jade Taylor (12)
Lostock Hall Community High School

Dad

I woke up in the middle of the night, by the noises on the stairs,
They're creaking and moaning, grumbling and groaning, slowly and in pairs.
A voice springs up loud and screaming and through the door I peer
And I yell, 'What are you doing? Stop! You can't just leave me here!'
I run through the room yelling, *'Stop!'*
I tear down the corridor, legs exploding until I reach the top.
The faster I run the more it hurts but down the steps I go
But stopped by the baby gate I yell, *'Stop, no!'*
I clamber over it, running through the rooms.
I run my fastest and see a light, a light in the room.
Through the kitchen I sprint, running very fast,
Now I'm running to the door not thinking of the past.
I pause to get some shoes on, slithering past a woman, anger on her face,
I spring through the steps, onto the stones, my heart setting the pace.
The faster I go it seems, even more true,
That I will never see him again, leaving me with no clue.
I tear through the yard, running at full speed,
I run through the gap in the fence, tucked by one reed,
I run into the street and see the light disappearing,
And suddenly I'm unaware of the ground nearing.
My face streaming, filled with tears,
Unable to put up with me, my mind fears.
You could have stopped it, but look back now,
Life's game, over another row.
I go back to the door vaguely aware
Of some woman sitting down, not one of a pair.
I traipse sadly through the living room,
Back up the stairs, through the corridor and into the gloom.
I get through the room, my face a picture of sad,
I climb into bed and I tearfully whisper, 'Dad.'

Matthew Tomlinson (13)
Lostock Hall Community High School

A Motorbike's Tale

Motorbikes that are sleeping soundly,
Are woken abruptly by their owners,
It is time for them to show the world,
They are not that different from us,
They can jump, leap and run around,
But differences do sometimes show,
Like death and hurt do not appear.

When they get out, they show the people
How they can ride the waves with strength,
Like a bull in its final minutes,
As well as being driven by pride,
But fear can get the better of them,
But after the storm there is always calm,
When the bikes are put back to sleep.

Although in fact their worries are not over,
As a new day brings a new situation,
Which also means a new solution
As the final draws closer and closer,
They just concentrate on the prize,
And when their time is almost finished,
They are put to rest for the final time.

Tom Smith (13)
Lostock Hall Community High School

Happy Or Sad

Are you happy or sad when the rain falls,
When the sun is shining,
When the wind is cold?

Are you happy or sad when the sun is out on a warm summer day,
When it's a cold winter's day,
When the leaves fall from the autumn trees?

Are you happy or sad when flowers bloom?
Teacher teaches and when the summer half term comes?

For some of these I am happy
But for some I am sad.

Lindsey Parker (12)
Lostock Hall Community High School

The Tiger

Swaying in the Indian breeze,
The tiger sleeps as it's sunny,
Not a sound can wake him,
Hunters wait, his skin is money.

Lying in the Indian sun,
The tiger, he is resting,
He can't be startled, nor awoken,
Hunters, start investing.

Hunting in the Indian grass,
The tiger, he is amazing,
He can't be watched, nor copied,
Hunters they watch gazing.

Eating in the Indian plain,
The tiger he is tired,
He simply cannot leap or run
Hunters' guns are fired.

Alexandra Jackson (12)
Lostock Hall Community High School

In The Desert

In the desert it's humid and bare,
Nothing to do, nothing to stare,
The sun beams down on the yellow hot sand,
It starts to burn my feet and hands.

In the desert it's calm and still
Nothing to keep you cold and chilled,
In the distance there's a single tree,
Birds are sitting in packs of threes.

In the desert there's plenty of animals,
Lots of insects but not many mammals,
Some of the animals are quiet and small
Some of the animals are loud and tall.

In the desert there's intelligent giraffes,
Eating, sleeping and bathing.
There they stand with spots so brown,
Why do I feel so low down?

In the desert there's tiny lizards,
They try to hide from the stormy blizzards,
All they do is change all day
Changing colours from green to grey.

In the desert it's like destiny
Everything is made up, imaginary,
Sometimes I wish I could come back here,
Maybe I will be next year.

Rebecca Farrell (13)
Lostock Hall Community High School

The Match

Waiting in my seat, anxiously for the players to come out,
So excited about what's going to happen.
People get up out of their seats and start cheering,
As Manchester United walk out alongside Wigan.

The referee blows his whistle and the game begins,
Each of the fans shouting abuse to the opponent.
The crowd soon calm down and it goes quiet
One fan makes a big shout of abuse and it all kicks off again.

The full time whistle blows
United have won the game two-one.
Singing with glory
Wigan walk away, hearts feeling heavy, off to the pub to drown their
sorrows.

Chelsey Roxburgh (14)
Lostock Hall Community High School

The Cats

It creeps around late at night,
Shrieking loudly, what a fright
Killing mice, eating birds
Stalking its territory
It comes inside in the morning
Looking so harmless
Purring and yawning.
Climbing on the bed and tapping you on the cheek
Sat by its dish waiting for its breakfast
Eyes of fire if you take too long
All it does is sleep and eat
Apart from at night where it wanders the streets
It climbs up big trees and gets itself stuck
A fireman comes to rescue it
Purring like a broken washing machine
Miaowing like a screaming kid
Its teeth come out when it's annoyed
Like horrible words that come out of children
Cute and cuddly cat
But is it?

Rebecca Gidley (12)
Lostock Hall Community High School

Leyland Warriors Is My Rugby Team

Leyland Warriors is my rugby team,
We could be the best team in the league.
We pass the ball all the time,
In order to get over the other team's try line.

When we win there's a huge cheer,
But if we lose the Cup Final there's many a tear.
If we lost at least we tried
After all our motto is, 'Play with Pride.'

Our team spirit is better than ever
My dad asks me if I want to join Chorley,
I say, 'Never!'

We score loads of tries
I kick loads of goals,
Our team's kit is black
It looks like coal.

I say to the boys, 'Keep your back foot on the line.'
We squash the other team like lemon and lime.

I love rugby; it's so much fun,
It keeps you fit,
Like a marathon run.
Leyland Warriors is my rugby team,
We are the best team in the league!

David Lonsdale (12)
Lostock Hall Community High School

The Incident

They stare at me with their evil eyes,
They think I did it to the boy that lies.
I see him there on the floor in front,
Why is it me they seem to hunt?
'It wasn't me that did it,' I cry,
But everyone thinks that's it's a lie.
I head for the office with great fear,
And then on my face I feel a tear.
I'm getting closer to the door,
And my footprints echo from the walls to the floor.
In front I see the door handle turn,
And then a voice saying, 'Young lady there is a lesson you must learn!'

Rachael Taylor (13)
Lostock Hall Community High School

Football

Running together to score a goal
The crowd goes wild
As I hit the ball
They all jump up with a big yes
They take the ball from out of their net
And kick it again
Then they kick-off
And we run for the ball
I go in for the slide
And take the ball
The player goes down
Then the crowd goes wild.

Lewis Miller (14)
Lostock Hall Community High School

Teddy

So now I come to you
To tell you what I've done
I tried to be good all day long
Until I spilled my milk
Mummy called me names and hit me awful hard
I know she loves me
She really does
You're my bestest friend teddy
I love you
Don't tell anyone what Mummy does
Or she will hit us both!

Michael Holland (12)
Lostock Hall Community High School

The Play-Off Final

Here it was, the time had come,
And I was all excited,
The play-off final was later on,
Against West Ham United.
Cardiff was a long way down,
I set off really early,
But if we were to win this game
We would have to win it fairly.
Cardiff was packed with lots of fans,
The two sides were mixed together,
If this was to be a Preston win,
It would go down in history forever.
It was coming to the end and we were one-nil down,
I knew it was almost impossible for us to get the play-off crown.
It was the final whistle,
In the West Ham end there were cheers,
But the PNE fans weren't happy at all,
We were all in tears.

Alex Cairns (13)
Lostock Hall Community High School

Goal!

The match verses Leyland St Mary's
Wasn't going very good,
The score was two-nil half-time,
But this was to Leyland St Mary's,
Lostock needed to get into shape for the second half.

The whistle went and the second half began,
Lostock had all the possession,
And eventually they got one goal back
They began to jump and cheer
They were saying, 'We're back in this game'
Lostock kept playing
They didn't give up hope
As their reward they got a second goal.

The clock was ticking
And Lostock wanted to win
As the last five minutes ticked
Anthony went on a run
Crossed it in good and Liam scored a head
Goal!
Three-two to Lostock, the crowd was going wild
The final whistle went and Lostock had won.

Ryan McManus (13)
Lostock Hall Community High School

My Favourite Place

My favourite place is where I feel at home,
Where I can do anything that I want.
My favourite place is so colourful,
It makes me smile and makes me happy.
I love the smell of the ocean and the sound.
This is where I want to be.
I lie there on the golden sandy beach,
And watch the dolphins leap into the sea.
When I'm here, I let my imagination float away like a bird.
My spirit is high, as I'm so excited.
I know I live here and belong here,
And this is true, I love this place.
The expression on people's faces when I tell them, it's priceless!
I know you may know this but some of you don't,
This is my favourite place and that is the Bahamas.

Kirstyn Winder (14)
Lostock Hall Community High School

Owl

The owl perched on a branch
Its eyes beaming headlights
Examining the earth.
Twigs and leaves rustle
The owl swoops down
Grabbing its prey
Gliding up it disappears
Gone!

The owl perched on a branch
Communicating with others
Its heart-shaped head turning
As noises distract him.
He glances left then right
Nothing in sight
He waits for his prey
A rustle!
A squeak!
Swoops down
Grabs . . .
Gone!

Emma-Louise Jedliczka (14)
Lostock Hall Community High School

I Just Want To Be The Real Me!

Sat here in the freezing cold.
I wrap my wet blanket round me.
People look and stare, I sit and beg.
I hear names being called to me.
I just want to be the real me!
I just wish I could go and hide.
I have no home and have no life.
Sitting out here all alone in the freezing cold.
I want a home.
I want a life.
All I feel like doing is crying.
I want to move on now after being like this for the last two years.
I just want to be the real me!
I don't know where my mum and dad are now.
Don't know what they look like.
They have probably seen me and acted as if they don't know me.
I hate my life.
I want it to be like everyone else.
I just want to be the real me!

Gemma Crook (13)
Lostock Hall Community High School

Bear Dancing

A small bear wanders freely in the forest,
Crying out for his friends,
But there is no reply,
So this bear walks freely by itself.

Hunters load up their guns,
Charging through the forest with not a care in the world,
They are looking for bears,
They capture them and use them for dancing to get money.

The bear does know
That the hunters are on their way,
The hunters have four Alsatians by their side,
They are fierce and mean.

It's dark in the box,
The bear is trapped, encased,
The hunters drive back to their hut
And attach a ring through its nose.

They box the bear up again
And drive him to the nearest town,
There they play music and make the bear dance.

Kimberley Rowe (13)
Lostock Hall Community High School

The Tiger

The tiger lies in deep brown sand
Camouflaged behind the tall grass.
Waiting for his prey to approach,
He sits still in the grass steady as a rock.
He tries to be as quiet as he can,
His breath's as short as possible.
The grass crunches as a deer chews,
The deer is now approaching.
He slowly moves step by step,
Silent like water floating,
The distance is now one metre,
As the tiger leaps up roaring
He pounces on the deer,
Claws out sharp as can be.
He takes a scratch at its belly,
The deer falls to the floor screeching.
He takes a bite,
He got what he wanted.
Roaring and scratching in the middle of a hot desert.
He finishes his afternoon meal,
He lies back and relaxes.
He spreads his legs wide open,
The tiger goes to sleep and sunbathes.

Rhianne Lealman (13)
Lostock Hall Community High School

My Hopes And Ambitions

I'd love to live a dream
I'd love to be a celebrity
Have my picture in magazines
I'll live my dreams.

I'd like to be a model
And stroll along the catwalk
I'll live my dreams.

I'd like to be a paramedic
Help save all those lives
I'll live my dreams.

I'd love to live a dream.

Georgina Chelton (13)
Lostock Hall Community High School

Filth

Hate this world
Destroy this world
One planet
One leader
Me!
Need to clean this world
Need to purify this world
Repair it back to before time
No war
No suffering
The war
The death
Destroyed by the power of hate
The hate of torture
The hate of pain
The hate of what we have now become.

Philip Whiteside (14)
Lostock Hall Community High School

My Cousin's Wedding

It was a long, exciting day
The trees were all blowing away
The wind was high
It would soon be night and emotions are flowing.

It was snowing and all were knowing
Of the greatest day in history
People were showing all sorts of colours
But soon, will she say yes? That's the mystery.

Little children play with toys
But soon they will pay for the noise
The groom is waiting with his heart in his head
Will the love of his life drop down dead!

His heart is pounding frantically
The doctor walks in to see his face
He says the news
His face fills with ace!

Heather Kaylow (14)
Lostock Hall Community High School

Guilty Conscience

Listening intently
Bang in the dead of night
Cat murmurs in fright
Lying alone in a dark dull room
Sitting up thinking this can't be true
I cannot sleep!

Go to the door, slam it shut
Open a window, look in disgust
I cannot sleep!

The dream I'd had was so real
Blood on the floor, looks like steel
Could this be
My guilty conscience haunting me?
I cannot sleep!

Flicker of light, all is good
Never have I felt so misunderstood
Going to sleep, all is good
Teachers haunting me isn't good
I can finally sleep!

Looking back at what I did
All for good
I'm not a kid
Telling me what they think
Breathing fire
I'm not giving in
I can finally sleep.

Daniel Walkingshaw (14)
Lostock Hall Community High School

Beauty

A dream,
An ambition,
My destiny yet to fulfil,
To save an animal species
Is all I wish to do.
A dream yet to come true,
For how do hunters do it?
Do their consciences not come into play?
How would they like
Their skins hung up on display?
A tiger's stripe,
A leopard's spot,
An elephant's great big tusk,
The beauty of an animal
Is more precious than one's money.

Craig Campbell (13)
Lostock Hall Community High School

Spring

Spring is the best of all.
It starts off cold, wet and lonely.
As it goes on it gets better and better.
Flowers start to grow.
Trees start to get their buds.
Winter has gone.
Spring is here.
Best season of the year.

Spring, spring.
That's its name.
Where the flowers start to blossom again.
The trees start to grow their leaves.
Spring is here.
Winter has gone.

Birds come back from the west.
Animals come out of hibernation.
The world is alive again.

Well now my poem is done.
Spring is here.
Winter has gone.

Abi Noon (13)
Lostock Hall Community High School

Bully

The sound of the bone break
The thud shook my brain
The dinner money I said he couldn't take
I don't know how he could be so vain.

The bully, his fist clenched and hard
The pain delivered forcefully
The tear of his face, I couldn't shake
It don't know how his heart could be so ice cold.

Daniel Titterington (14)
Lostock Hall Community High School

Through The Rain

The wind blowing in my mane
Walking through high grass
Trotting with my long tail swaying
Trotting on a racetrack
Galloping through flowers
Rolling around in wet mud!

The rain droplets on my coat
My shimmering wispy fair
Blowing and giving me a chill
The rain droplets fall as I stretch my limbs
Through the damp air, hooves shining
Catching the sun's rays
My long lush tail flickering
In the water's reflection.

Melissa Dickinson (14)
Lostock Hall Community High School

An Animal

I am sliding across the grass
Moving as fast as I can
Feeling tired, the sun as hot as ever
Trying to reach my friends and family
Slithering across the brown crunchy leaves
I was so close to my home now
Home sweet home
But then I was caught by a shadow
I couldn't get away quick enough
Then I ended up somewhere bright and mysterious
This place is Heaven!
Today when I died in the darkness
That was the end of my snail life.

Rebecca Gardner (12)
Lostock Hall Community High School

Butterfly

It brushed across my cheek
As I lay there in the grass,
The sun was blazing down on me
And I wondered where it would go next.
Where, where, where did it go?
The beautiful butterfly that I just saw!

I saw it again, there before me,
I tried to catch it
But it flew off into the distance,
There it goes,
Where, where, where did it go?
The colourful butterfly that I just saw!

It landed again on the flower,
But it looked different from the one before.
Was it the same one?
No, it's not, there are so many.
Where, where, where did it go?
The gorgeous butterfly that I just saw!

Rebecca McLaughlin (12)
Lostock Hall Community High School

The Swinging Singer

She strutted to the crowd,
People roaring like lions
She took two gulps of air
As she raised her microphone.

As the loud clash banged,
She began to sing a song,
Her voice was superb
She started to dance.

As the singer danced around,
People made a lot of sound,
Her fans cheered a lot,
As she was praised like she was God.

She was trapped by guards
Alone inside,
Her head stood with pride,
But her soul sank like a boat.

After the song,
The crowd cheered,
She stood tall and proud,
But felt awfully down.

She felt really low,
Lower than the floor,
Her face looked like she was happy,
She must hurt inside
But she's a swinging singer.

Alice Corrigan (12)
Lostock Hall Community High School

Remember The Sadness

Whistling, whistling,
Faster than light,
No one can see it,
Nobody.

Whistling, whistling,
Racing through rivers,
Pounding round the bend,
Dashing.

But yet, the sadness
Of the whistling.
The eyes of the monster,
Howling.
I see the broken heart,
Moving, slowly.
No one deserves this
At all.

The trespassing of the wind
Makes rivers flood.
Only very few
Survive.

Rapids, beating faster than eyesight,
Hitting people as they go to a watery grave.
No one can help,
Nobody.

I stand alone, dreaming,
Dreaming of what the world could be.
I am alone, waiting,
Silent as the owl at night.
A tear drops from sight as the wind blows
Nothing can prepare me for the days I have left.

Samantha Ackers (12)
Lostock Hall Community High School

Death

Staring me in my eyes
The fear of laughter and lies
It's all around me so I can't see
What can I do to set me free?
Desperately trying to keep my sanity
I'm a prisoner within my own worries
They all hate me or so I think
I know it, do it, drop and fall
Life means nothing to me anymore
The pain is growing, it must end soon
Cascading, plummeting through the night sky
This is it, here is my death
The pain is growing more and more
I'll never use his name in vain
If only he could help me stop the pain.

Matthew Bird (12)
Lostock Hall Community High School

The Great Outdoors

The elephant lies in the midday sun
Listening intently for the sound of a gun,
For his great tusks are worth a hefty price
Although nothing costs more than taking a life.

All of a sudden he hears a loud crack
So the animal got up and tried to turn back
He pounded on and on he tried
And then he felt a bullet in his side.

The animal fell onto the hard, dusty floor
But all he heard was the sound of a door
Then he saw the man on the bank
Crack and all he saw was blank.

Edward Worsley (12)
Lostock Hall Community High School

My Daddy

He swears, he shouts, he crashes, he bangs,
Daddy, why do you do this?
'Shut up!' he screams.
I beg for forgiveness but no,
He hurts, he trembles, I cry,
He lunges out, I flee to the floor,
Again I shout, 'Daddy, why do you do this?'
'Where's Mummy?' Me sprawled on the floor,
'Don't Daddy, don't, I love you!'
I wonder and wonder why he does it,
Thoughts running over and over in my head,
'Daddy, what have I done to deserve this?'
He heads for the kitchen, I run to the door,
I sprint to my room like a ghost of fear,
I hide in my wardrobe,
I cannot see,
He does not come and get me.
I sit there in pain, it's hurting me,
I fall asleep to never see,
Why my daddy killed me.

Gemma McCarthy (12)
Lostock Hall Community High School

Golden Eagle

High up in the morning cliffs,
Screeching and searching,
Hunting and diving,
Leaping off jagged edges,
Flapping and looking,
Gliding and shifting,
Airbound without a sound,
Secret and unfound,
Soaring with ease through the sky,
Smaller creatures passing by,
A sharp eye glimpses at movement,
Sharp claws like daggers,
Never crossing the far line,
Feathers worth an expensive lot,
Fall to the ground below,
As it perched in a tree
Just where it would usually be,
Eying at its newfound prey,
It would dive and swoop.
Grasp and at last
Weakened with despair,
Bloodshot eyes and flapping wings,
A small bird sings for mercy.
Loaded onto the back of a truck,
No longer to be screeching or searching,
But perched above a chamber door
Staring, not moving, for evermore.

Heather Blundell (12)
Lostock Hall Community High School

The Silent Bully

He creeps on you like prey
As if you're his dinner now
The silence of his big hits
It's how he got his name.

Threats come out one by one
Every hour of the day
'Don't tell anyone or I'll hit you harder again!'
So they took it in and hoped for the best.

Then one day a bigger bully
Came to school that day
The silent bully didn't like that
And hit him on the head.

It knocked him out
With such force and power
And he ended up
In a hospital dying.

So the silent bully
Was no longer silent
With a bad record
And no longer violent.

Matthew Galland (12)
Lostock Hall Community High School

The Poppy Field

In the poppy field it was quiet,
Bunnies hopping round,
Then the bunnies ran away,
And men were firing guns,
Bang! Bang!

Men were killed and wounded,
Families were crying,
But one day the gun firing stopped,
Because all the men were dead,
Their bodies were like polka dots all over the ground.

Then the bunnies came back
The poppies filled the field once more,
Everyone was happy because there was no war.

Aimee Dunderdale (12)
Lostock Hall Community High School

A Soldier

A soldier will march,
A soldier will learn,
A soldier will battle for his country.

A soldier will fight,
A soldier will kill,
A soldier will battle for his country.

A soldier is brave,
A soldier is courageous,
A soldier is ready for anything.

A soldier will see death,
Death of a friend,
Death of an enemy.

Shooting and firing,
Shelling and killing,
All these a soldier has to see and do.

A soldier will know
One wrong move and
His life will finish
And he will be no more.

Iain Jardine (12)
Lostock Hall Community High School

He Lies In Bed

He lies in bed, staring at the ceiling, wondering what she's doing.
He loves her like no other, pure and honest to life.
She asks herself why hasn't he asked me, asked me what love is.
Everyone can see the bond growing between them, except themselves.
She loves him.
He too is besotted.

Xandrina Allday (12)
Lostock Hall Community High School

My School Poem

Assembly is the first thing in my day,
The teachers have a lot to say!
Science, maths and English too,
In the lessons I don't have a clue.
Division and nouns are going through my head,
I just want to go home and go to bed.
But later on we have PE,
Football, netball and dancing, *yippee!*
Even though music and drama are good,
I still get embarrassed and go as red as blood!

Now it's lunchtime, I sit with my gang,
People rush past with trays, *crash, bang!*
Then we go outside and have a chat,
But balls zoom past and end with a splat.
Next up, we have history,
The Romans and Vikings are such a mystery.

Next up, my class has art,
Now, that's the creative part.
Some French words are hard to make out,
'Bonjour! Ca Va!' I shout.
Although school is fun and usually cheery,
When I get home I'm very weary!

Lauren Whittaker (12)
Mount Carmel RC High School

PE Rap

PE is such a fabulous thing
Shame we can't wear all of ze bling.
Cos we have to wear loadz of rubbish
It makes me mate look like a fish.
Mi teacher is quite funny
His two front teeth look like those of a bunny.
As we play football so joyful and fun
He sits there, so need to run.
We run about n pass ze ball
N most of ze time, we score a goal.
Me n mi mates play for ze team
When we concede we burst with steam.
So as you can see PE is brill
After PE all we do is chill!

Samuel Cox (12)
Mount Carmel RC High School

My Sock

I woke up at ten o'clock
And jumped out of my bed in a shock.
I started to scream
This must be a dream.
School has started and I can't find my sock
I searched high and low, here and there.
I couldn't find it anywhere.
I asked my mum and she said,
'Get a new pair and go to bed.'
'But Mum today is Monday.'
'No, it's only Sunday.'
I went to my room with only one sock
And then I heard a tick-tock.
I looked up high and started to cry
It was hanging from the clock.
My mum walked in and said, 'I told you to go to bed.'
'But Mum you see I found my sock
I'll celebrate instead.'
I danced with that sock all night
We made an excellent pair
Until I found another one lying on my chair!

Clifford Appleby & Nicholas Marcinkowski (12)
Mount Carmel RC High School

My PC Isn't Working

My PC isn't working,
There's a virus knocking 'bout,
I need to sort it quickly,
Before the lights go out.

It's lurking in there somewhere,
I'll find it like the rest,
It's just a shame I don't have Sophos,
To help me in my quest.

I'll find it and destroy it
So the lesson has been learned,
You need a virus-free computer,
When there's CDs to be burned!

Ross Butterly (12)
Mount Carmel RC High School

Drama Commotion

As Shakespeare said, 'The world's a stage'
So carry on reading my front page.
We were in a drama,
We were on emotion,
It was causing such a commotion.
Then it was time for me and ma script an' on the way up I totally
tripped!
What happened next you don't wanna know,
Instead just listen to ma rhythm and flow.
All I want is an audience to come an' watch ma great performance!

Alexandra Preugschat (12)
Mount Carmel RC High School

Being A Cat Is Hard!

Weave between my master's legs,
And tickle his feet while he's asleep,
It's so hard to hunt for food,
Just miaow and look real cute.

Sleep all day and hunt all night,
I give the hunted such a fright,
Sometimes I let them get away
To hunt again another day.

I groom my fur,
I lick and preen,
It's such hard work,
To make it clean.
It's hard being a cat, miaow!

Naomi Bury (11)
Mount Carmel RC High School

DT

DT is the best
It's just so good
It's better than the rest.

Wood and plastic using tools
You can't use them if you're a fool.

Dangerous machines, beware
If you are not, they will give you a scare!

Mr Stobbs and Mr Clarke
When they talk they sound like they bark.

Once you have finished and tidied up
You will have something to win you a cup.

James Kelly (13)
Mount Carmel RC High School

Come On Rovers!

Shout for the Blues,
We're going to make it through!
Rovers are going to win,
Then let's begin.

Come on Rovers!
We need to move up!
Come on Rovers!
Win the cup!

We will fight to the end,
Sailing through each round.
We are the champions!
Let's bring it to the ground.

Come on Rovers!
We'll cheer for you every day.
Come on Rovers!
Show that quality play.

The fans are here,
We'll cheer you on.
We'll walk a lot of miles
When you win, the other fans are gone.

Come on Rovers!
We need to score a goal.
Come on Rovers!
We'll eat a meat pie through it all.

The final whistle is approaching,
What are we going to do?
Pederson scores a goal!
That's it, we're through.

Come on Rovers!
Thanks a lot Mark Hughes.
Come on Rovers!
We are the Blues.

Daniel McLaughlin (12)
Mount Carmel RC High School

This Feeling

It may not seem real,
It may not make much sense,
But this feeling inside
Is getting harder to hide.
I shut my eyes to blank you out,
But your outline is still there,
I try harder not to stare
But you stand beautifully
With your blonde hair.
You may think I'm stupid,
You may think I'm wrong,
But this feeling inside,
Is unbelievably strong.
I may be different,
I may be occupied,
But this love I share for you
I'm caught down, I'm tied.
It may not seem the time,
It may not seem the place,
It may not seem appropriate,
It may seem a race.
But time is running out,
Time ticks by,
But when this poem ends
I've got to say goodbye.

Ellie Hawkins (12)
Mount Carmel RC High School

Peace

Be thankful for what you have,
Don't leave someone out because of the colour of their skin
Or the way they choose to dress.
There are other ways in order to impress one and another.
Charisma is the art of intelligence.
Elegance is the skill to approach another to make each other feel at
ease.
Peace is all that we need and all that we ask of each other.

There's no point in getting yourself into a bother about it.
Try and then let it go, it just goes to show the bigger being.
It's all about seeing the ways round the tricky bends.
Sometimes we may need to pretend to extend quality relationships.
In the end friendships that are built on steady grounds will be ones that
are found.
So be proud of who and what you are and where you are from.
Take it from the bottom and stretch it all the way to the top.
There's no way we can afford life to be a flop.
Be thankful. Think about what you have and not what you don't have.
Be thankful. Be sure of what you say before you speak,
Be aware that you not the only one there.
Be thankful of what you have at least.

Sophia Ali (17)
Oldham Sixth Form College

My Beach!

As I place my foot on the smooth, hot sand,
The birds tweet like they're talking.
The sun shines on the deep blue sea
As I put one foot in front of the other.
As I carry on walking I can smell chips on the pier
The fresh sea air fills my lungs.
As I look up the sky is light blue,
There's not a cloud in the sky.

As I look forward I can see the sun setting,
Lots of colours mix together,
Ruby red, violent violet and luscious lemon,
Then the colours fade.
The night goes black and the stars and moon come out,
The stars shine on the sea and then it goes blank and it's time to come
back.

Hannah Yates (12)
Our Lady's Catholic College

Football Mad

The whistle blows
Ryan has the ball with space
He passes to a defender
With a lot of pace.

His teammate Oliver
Hits the post
Because he is sure
He saw a ghost.

The whistle blows
It's a free kick
He steps up to take it
But gets hit with a brick.

Ryan gets the ball
He is in the box
A defender tries to tackle him
But he is a sly as a fox.

Eighty-nine minutes
The manager is having a fret
Ryan kicks the ball
It's in the back of the net.

Ryan Leonard (12)
Our Lady's Catholic College

Jailbird

The door goes *thud!*
The vase goes *boom!*
As Fredric Wilson enters the room.
The room went silent
As he sat down,
Upon his face he had a frown.
They all whimpered,
He just stared,
They wanted to know how he had faired.
They asked him and he said,
'I'll tell you later,' as he stormed out.
The door went *thud!*
The car wheels screeched.
As he went speeding down the street
The moral of this poem is
Take a deep, deep breath
And tell them all of your rest
In the jailbird's nest.

Daymeon Clemance (12)
Our Lady's Catholic College

The Snowman

The sky is blue
But who knew
Everyone did,
Everyone did.
Except Sid.
Sid heard of the sky being blue
But he started to cry
Because he had to say goodbye
To the big blue sky.
The sky is blue
But who knew
Everyone did,
Everyone did
So did Sid.

Yoko Jackson (13)
Our Lady's Catholic College

Shopping

I go to town every week,
To look for clothes that fit me sleek.
When I'm bored on Saturday.
I phone my mates and I'm on my way.
Looking in them fancy shops,
People in trouble with the cops.
Shops with food, books and clothes
Shops with perfume, I like those!
My friend found these shoes and decided to buy,
She said, 'You would suit them, why don't you try?'
I put them on and walked around the shop,
With those high-heeled shoes went clippety-clop!
Now it is time to stop,
So I ring my mum to pick me up,
She asks me what I've bought
'Come on, let's have a look!'

Charlotte Kilifin (12)
Our Lady's Catholic College

The Dog

He was a dog walking in the fog
A fat ugly dog chewing on a frog
As he walked through the fog
He saw a warthog lying in the fog
He gave him a snog with a mouth full of frog.

Oliver Parsons (12)
Our Lady's Catholic College

Reckless Ron

Reckless Ron is now dead and gone
One day he didn't look and got hit by an ice cream truck.
On the road were blood and guts,
Liquorice, screwballs and hazelnuts.
Mr Whippy, the ice cream man
Got told off by the police and got a ten-year ban.
Now he can't sell 99s because he got a mighty fine,
Off he went to his old job
Selling cars for his boss Bob.
Mr Bob was so awfully mean
To his workers he was a big monstrous fiend.
Ten years later Mr Whippy broke out
'I'm an ice cream man again,' he would shout.

Jordan Whittle (12)
Our Lady's Catholic College

Winter Feeling

W inter is a cold season; it snows almost every day,
I n my house in front of the fire
N earer and nearer the snow inches
T ime is ticking, snow is falling.
E very drop of white cold snow
R acing to the ground, sticking.

F leece on, hood up, warm clothes, I'm ready to go
E ating my way to the door
E xcitingly opening the door
L ight bright snow on my feet
I n my hair
N earer I get to the field
G etting snowballs, having fights, that's a winter feeling.

Charlotte Winder (12)
Our Lady's Catholic College

England

England is a great nation
We invented the train station
Don't forget eggs and bacon
We're English not Jamaican.

England is the land of free
With wildlife like the bee
Buildings ever so tall
We've even got a shopping mall.

Joseph Sailor (12)
Our Lady's Catholic College

The Jungle

What's hiding in the trees and long grass?
Could it be a lion waiting for its prey to pass
Or a tiger who's waiting for its dinner to come?
Tell the other animals to run, run, run!
A flock of birds fly overhead
Because they fear they may be dead
If the hunter gets them with his gun
Shooting up high towards the sun.
All the animals run, run, run!
The sun has gone down safe at last
Time to sleep and play and fast
See to the babies, everyone fed,
Tucked up in the grass, it's time for bed,
Sleep, sleep, sleep.

Paul Metcalfe (12)
Our Lady's Catholic College

Tigers

Roar! Roar!
The tiger goes out in a jungle or desert plain
He stalks, thinks through the long weedy grass, waiting, waiting for
lunch to come
Into the fray, but wait, what's that out there?
The tiger thought, *why, it's a young water buffalo by itself all alone,*
No friends to comfort him, I'm hungry, I could eat an African elephant,
whole!
Do I take the chance?
Yes, I'll take the chance,
Right, check, creep, check, creep, stop, wait, wait, check, creep, is it in
range . . .
Yes it is!
Judge the distance is it close, far, close, now for the kill!

Lee Hawkesford (12)
Our Lady's Catholic College

Shopping

Shopping is fun,
Shopping is great,
Shopping is something I do with my mate.
I shop for shoes,
I shop for clothes,
I shop for almost any of those.
I'll shop until I drop,
Then rest for a while and
Start again another day.

Danielle Graham (13)
Our Lady's Catholic College

Cricket

Cricket is an English game
You throw the ball again and again
You hit the ball go for a six
Don't forget your Weetabix.

Catch the ball, shout, *'Howzat!'*
Watch Michael Vaughan throw his bat
Watch the bowler come running in
Lets go of the ball and watch it spin.

Now it's time for you to bat
Grab your helmet, take off your hat
Take your guard, check the field
When you win grab the trophy shield.

Sam Heron (12)
Our Lady's Catholic College

The People Inside

On my way home
I dare not walk past
The graveyard
On my local park path.

It is not the rotting gravestones
That scares me, nor the gloomy light,
But it is the eerie people lingering inside.

It is those six feet under,
The ones that are dead,
They fill me with fear
And also with dread.

As I walk along that lonely park path,
I can just imagine them coming slowly from the ground,
And dragging their undead feet along behind me.

And so that is why I fear them
The reason why I dread
It's not the weathered gravestones
Nor the gloomy light
But the eerie, undead people
Lingering inside.

Alex Lewis (13)
Rossall School

Fire Mountain

Looming, sinister, dark and cold,
Bleak, hard and forbidding,
A worn and craggy mountain top
Reaches up into the clouds.

Where the raging sea meets the storm-tossed sky,
Where the thunder's crash
And the lightning's flash
Is the only light to see by.

Deep inside the mountain's heart
There lurks an eerie glow,
The glow of scarlet, gleaming eyes
That beam out dread and woe.

The livid eyes, the glinting fangs,
The curved and sharpened jaws,
The sparkle of scale on snake-like tail,
The grind of hungry claws.

The beast, he shook his horn-wreathed head
And stretched his wings outside,
And from his throat a mighty roar
Could be heard from far and wide.

The hillside shook, the ocean trembled,
The mountain groaned in pain
As lava gushed out of its top
Like blood, or deadly rain.

The ash was billowed in the sky
And blocked out all the sun,
The scorching lava slowly cooled,
The dragon's work was done.

Bethany Sullivan (13)
Rossall School

Footsteps

Footsteps, footsteps call a warning,
The shadows try to make a sound.
The darkness wraps around the figure
Like a finger round a hand.

And as I wait for her silhouette
To return from the dark loom
I feel a presence getting closer
And I'm worried for her doom.

A flash of red collapsed on me
As dizziness took control
I tried to call out and warn the maiden
But alas I heard her fall.

As I entered the monster's mouth
I shivered. The wall was wet
I took a sniff and wandered closer
But it was only darkness that I met.

Charlotte Byrne (13)
Rossall School

Sanare, Sanatarium . . .

She wrapped her arms around you
And whispered in those ears
Something too tiring to listen to,
Something too hard to comprehend,
Something she possibly shouldn't have said,
But, you see,
When you know of this,
It's miserable to keep in.

Those submissive little eyes shimmered,
Of green and unsettled peace,
Unsettled slightly, unsettled once gone,
Because she knew what button to touch
To take that pain away.
And you had to,
She'd said, had to know,
Just before your hands turned cold, she'd said,
'I love you far too much . . .'

She'd thought those ears couldn't,
Shouldn't comprehend.
She'd thought those orbs just couldn't,
Maybe wouldn't understand.
They shouldn't have shimmered,
Perhaps, shouldn't have glimmered,
Those eyes unfocused, these fingers
Stirred,
And our words fused . . .

Swie-Joo Liem (13)
Rossall School

Midnight Alleyway

Walking down the alleyway
Darkness all around.
The screech of car tyres,
The eerie midnight sounds.

A clunk in the doorway,
You try to run away.
A clang in the alleyway,
Oh, why do you stay?

What's that in the background?
Footsteps from behind.
You try to turn around,
Turn around to find.

A man dressed in black,
An eerie atmosphere.
You try to scream and shout,
But are overcome with fear.

You feel an arm grasp your shoulder,
And a cold wind blow by.
You hear a scream in the night
A ghostly baby's cry.

In a silent whisper,
The man begins to say,
'Excuse me Mam, but can you tell me where I am?
I've seemed to have lost my way.'

And so you reply and answer
And the man goes on his way,
And so you continue walking
Down the alleyway.

Walking down the alleyway,
Darkness all around.
The screech of car tyres,
The eerie midnight sounds.

James Harkness (13)
Rossall School

Millionaire Woman

Morning and millionaire woman wakes up
To the sound of gentle moving water in her head
The soft rays of sun on her skin.

Beautiful birds and people sunbathing on the beach below
The stunning green sea surrounding the perfect view
She always comes back
Groggily, groggily comes back to sounds of bustling people
To surge of pens to paper, to dull school life
Muffling, muffling her crumpled sheets wave
Millionaire woman lifts her head, another same old day.

Becky Williams (15)
Sharples School

Multibillionaire Woman

Morning and multibillionaire woman wakes up to the sound of a Hoover
motor
Back and forth pushed by her cleaner.
The remnants of last night's party all over the room.
In the room, darkened by the closed curtains,
Shapes of multicoloured balloons swaying slightly in the breeze from
the open window
She always comes back, groggily, groggily,
Comes back to the commotion of a busy family household,
To shouting voices, to noisy neighbours
Muffling, muffling her ageing mattress creaks
As multibillionaire woman rises, another school day.

Kayleigh Hanna (15)
Sharples School

Rock Star Man

Gig time
Rock star man rocks on to the sound of roaring fans
Buzz of guitar
And the rhythmic beating of drums.

Towers of fire
Lying on the palms of fans
Dripping with sweat
Back on stage
Ready to rock again
But I come back groggily, groggily.

Come back to roaring cars outside
My buzzing headache
Rhythm beating of my alarm,
Mumbling, mumbling
Lying on the covers of my bed, heave to my feet
Another normal day.

Thomas Wolfenden (15)
Sharples School

Singer

Morning and singer wakes up to the sound of joyous fans in his head,
The piercing whistles and cheers.
Partygoers and surfers setting out to the beach to ride the waves,
The golden sands gleaming at him from the beach of his dream house.
He always comes back groggily, groggily,
Comes back to the rain of a miserable and gloomy afternoon,
To the sound of traffic, to dull mournful weather.
Muffling, muffling, crumpled duvet,
Singer heaves himself, another bottom day.

Nadeem Mogra (15)
Sharples School

Billionaire Man

Morning and billionaire man wakes up to the sound of the majestic eagle
Calling all in his dream the steady rush of wings beating, beating.
Strange koala bears and his mansion imposing upon the landscape.
The marble floor sparkling in the steady sun on the beaches of Australia.
He wakes up his mind, he's cloudy, groggily, groggily.
Comes back to his eagle in the form of jet-black crow.
Back to rain and muddy grounds, back to smoggy motorway,
Choking, choking, his covers dragged off,
Billionaire man heaves himself, another bottom day.

Matthew Hackett (15)
Sharples School

New York Woman

Morning and New York woman wakes up to the sound of cars and
streets in her head
The constant buzz of conversation.

High-heeled shoes and people hurrying to work
The sun glinting off skyscrapers from the east of Manhattan Island
She always comes back
Grumpily, grumpily
Comes back to sounds of a crowded school corridor
To the scratching of pens to boring Sharples School

Snoring, snoring
Her pencil case pillow
New York woman wakes herself, another school day.

Emma Swift (15)
Sharples School

Midnight

As my steed cantered o'er the frosty hills,
I heard a heart-rending howl, then silence.
The silence was disturbing, I made my horse trot fast.
All of a sudden I see,
A flash of black streaking across the moon,
A hearty cackle of triumph travels to my ears.
A slight hiss and a black cat with emerald green eyes steps forth,
Out of the rambling undergrowth.
Streaked towards a house.
I had not seen this house before I set eyes on the cat.
My horse's hooves crunched as they met the icy ground.
As we approached the house, it suddenly reared,
Sending frost flying across the wild garden.
The frost flew in yet I could not see until we were halfway home.
By that time my horse had calmed and trotted quietly.
Back across the frosty fields
Even now I hear a throaty cackle, and a slight hiss intrudes my dreams.

Ayesha Martin **(11)**
Sharples School

Fireworks

Whizz, whoosh, whizz, whoosh
They all go off at night
Bang, pop, bang, pop
They make the sky so bright.

Sizzle, crack, sizzle, crack
It sounds like a bomb has come
Bang, pop, bang, pop
Finally the fireworks have done.

Shannan Luntley (11)
Sharples School

Hallowe'en

Spooky spiders crawl
Wicked witches laugh
Glowing pumpkins watch
Trick or treating children
Howling wolves call
Purring cats creep
Bloodthirsty Dracula spies
Haunted castle stands
White skeletons rattle
Zombies awake from the dead
Squeaking rats nibble
Oo, o noises echo from the ghost.

Laura Formston (11)
Sharples School

The Hawk

The hawk is great,
It is never late.
Its wings are big,
In the air it does a jig.
But before it hits the ground,
It twirls around.
Then it swoops up at the last second
And then it gets beckoned
By her mother
To come and play with her brother.
But she does not enjoy this,
So she signals she'll give it a miss.
Now it is time to go to bed
Anyway, that's what her brother said.

Jacob Fear (11)
Sharples School

One Summer Day

One summer day
Everything was fine,
When I got a dog
And the dog was mine.

He was cute and sweet
And was lots of fun
And he liked to go out
And play in the sun.

He liked to jump
Around everywhere,
Soaring, swooping
Through the air.

I used to greet him
By rubbing his back,
And then he'd go back
Down for a nap.

One summer's day
Everything was fine,
When I got a dog
And the dog was mine.

Bethany Jarvis (11)
Sharples School

School Rules

Put your hand up,
Don't call out,
Sit up straight,
And please don't shout.

Listen with your ears,
Don't talk with your mouth,
Because the teacher is here
And she's going to shout.

If you don't want detention,
You better pay attention,
And if you follow these rules
You won't be one of the fools.

Ameera Mogra (11)
Sharples School

Post

I post my post,
I post it every day,
I post my post,
I post it to my mum.

I post, I post,
Why do I post?
I post, I post,
For my mum every day.

I post, I post,
I post every day,
I post, I post,
I post it to my mum.

Aamina Patel (11)
Sharples School

Bubble Bath

The bubbles go everywhere
I dodge them in my lair
I see them everywhere
Then I notice they are not there.

So the bubbles are gone
I still see a figure of three
At the moment they are going free
And touching me.

Look at the last one I see myself
I see a reflection and everything else
Then *pop* goes my bubble.

Then I get in my bath
Bubbles shoot all over the place
Not caring more like swerving
So once again
The bubbles are everywhere
So I dodge them in my lair.

Brad Knowles (11)
Sharples School

The Devil's Rockets

Upon this spooky night
We unleash the rockets of fright
In the ground
They silently wait as if spellbound
These terrific idols stand and wait
Until they all unleash their bombing fate.

All of these things are tired of slumber
But soon the flame comes hunting under
Soon the flame goes to the end
The devils fly up to the sky they send
And with a glittering explosion sends them on their way
Before the end of the world comes today.

Ben Hilton (11)
Sharples School

Tranquillity

In a lock of peaceful sleep
The wild birds set her free
The cool sea breeze waves in
A mirror to the sky.
Feet sink into hot golden snow
Sun bouncing off the glazing sea
The tickling tide touches her toes
As tranquil setting takes hold again.
She strolls up and down, soles bare
Takes in deep sea air,
She settles into the cotton hammock
Creating pictures of fashion and style.

Alarm bells ring at 7am
Hit the snooze just one more time
A true British morning welcome
With no sand, sea or sun.

Rosa O'Byrne (15)
Sharples School